# Those Invisible Spirits Called Angels

## by RENALD E. SHOWERS

**The Friends of Israel Gospel Ministry, Inc.**
**P. O. Box 908, Bellmawr, NJ 08099**

*Bethel Baptist Church*
P.O. BOX 167
AUMSVILLE, OR  97325

# THOSE INVISIBLE SPIRITS CALLED ANGELS

Renald E. Showers

Copyright© 1997 by The Friends of Israel Gospel Ministry, Inc.
Bellmawr, New Jersey 08099

**Second Printing** ...................................**2002**

All rights reserved. Printed in the United States of America. No part of this book may be reproduced, stored in a retrieval system, or transmitted, in any form or by any means, electronic, mechanical, photocopying, recording, or otherwise, without the prior written permission of the publisher. For information, address The Friends of Israel Gospel Ministry Inc., P.O. Box 908, Bellmawr, NJ 08099.

Library of Congress Catalog Card Number: 96-61712
ISBN 0-915540-24-X

Cover by Left Coast Designs, Portland, OR

Visit our Web site at *www.foi.org*

# TABLE OF CONTENTS

Introduction ................................................................4

Chapter 1   The Existence, Number, and Nature of Angels....6

Chapter 2   The Council, Ranks, and Designations
            of Angels.................................................24

Chapter 3   The Relationships of Angels to
            Human Beings......................................46

Chapter 4   The Relationships of Angels to
            Jesus Christ.........................................51

Chapter 5   The Fall of Angels .............................76

Chapter 6   No Salvation for Fallen Angels ........114

Chapter 7   The Dwelling Places and Judgments
            of Angels............................................119

Chapter 8   Activities of Holy Angels ................124

Chapter 9   Activities of Evil Angels..................141

Chapter 10  The Angel of the Lord .....................157

# INTRODUCTION

For many years in the modern world, some people scoffed at the idea of angels. They believed that the concept of angels was started by poor, ignorant people in the Dark Ages who were susceptible to wild imaginations, and that the intelligent people of the modern, enlightened age knew better than to accept such fantasies. As a result, they asserted that belief in the existence of such supernatural beings was a superstition that needed to be rejected.

During those same years, the majority of people could not have cared less about angels. Many were totally oblivious to the existence of these beings. Others could not be bothered with thoughts about something that seemed to have no practical relevance to their daily lives.

By contrast, today the world is experiencing an excessive fascination with angels. The 1990s have witnessed an explosion of books, articles, images, pins, pictures, television programs, comic strips, and films about angels. Even such secular publications as *Time* and *Newsweek* magazines have noted this renewed interest in the subject.

There are at least two negative consequences of this new attraction. First, much of what has been produced in conjunction with this trend is inaccurate and misleading. Second, for some people, excessive fascination with angels has become almost all-consuming.

The Bible is the only accurate, authoritative source of information on the subject of angels because its ultimate author is God, the creator and sovereign Lord of the angels. The Bible contains considerable revelation concerning these spirit beings.

The fact that the Scriptures present this revelation reveals that

God wants human beings to be aware of the existence of angels, to possess accurate knowledge of them, and to avoid the two extremes of past years, which either denied their existence or could not care less about them.

In addition, the biblical revelation clearly demonstrates that angels are not the supreme beings of the universe. They are only creatures, subject to the personal, sovereign God, and are never to be worshiped. They are servants of God and even serve human beings. Through this revelation, the Bible makes God—not angels—the major focus of its attention. Thus, it avoids the new extreme fascination with angels and signifies that such fascination is misplaced and wrong.

Because the Bible avoids all of these extremes, we can conclude that it presents a balanced view of angels. Human beings are to possess the accurate knowledge presented in the Scriptures concerning these spirit beings, but they are not to be excessively fascinated with them. Because God is the ultimate author of the Bible, we can further conclude that this balanced view is correct.

This book attempts to faithfully present the biblical revelation concerning angels. It is my hope that this exposition of that revelation will help readers acquire the Bible's balanced view.

—Renald Showers

# 1

# THE EXISTENCE, NUMBER, AND NATURE OF ANGELS

## The Existence of Angels

The Bible clearly presents the existence of angels as reality. At least three facts indicate this. First, 34 of the 66 books of the Bible—more than half—refer to angels by the simple term "angel" (singular and plural), and they refer to them in ways that imply their existence. It is interesting to note that 17 of these books are located in the Old Testament, and 17 are in the New Testament. Thus, the witness is evenly divided between the testaments.

Second, the simple term "angel" (singular and plural) occurs more than 300 times in the Bible. In addition to these occurrences, the Scriptures refer to angelic beings by other terms, such as "cherubim," "seraphim," "archangel," "prince," "sons of

God," "power of the air," "principalities," "powers," "rulers of the darkness of this world," "spiritual wickedness in high places," "thrones," and "dominions." Thus, through the numerous usages of all these terms, the Bible places considerable emphasis on these beings. In light of this, the existence of angels cannot be lightly brushed aside.

Third, Jesus Christ referred to angels frequently and in a way that made it obvious that He believed in their existence. For example, He talked about the relationship of angels to children (Mt. 18:10), declared that He could have more than twelve legions of angels at His disposal to protect Him from His enemies (Mt. 26:53), and indicated that angels will attend and serve Him at His Second Coming (Mt. 13:39-41; 16:27; 24:30-31; 25:31). To deny the existence of angels is to pose a serious problem concerning the character and truthfulness of Jesus Christ. If He was not accurate in His comments about angels, how can we be certain that He was accurate in other areas of His teaching? For those who believe that Jesus Christ is the eternal Son of God incarnated in human flesh, His statements concerning angels are conclusive with regard to their existence.

## The Number of Angels

How many angels are there? The Bible does not give us a total number. No matter how much you search the pages of the Bible, you will never find a statement such as, "There are 2,369,758,219 angels."

In spite of the fact that the Scriptures do not give a total figure, they do make it clear that there is an *enormous* host of angelic beings. The Apostle John (Rev. 5:11) saw "ten thousand times ten thousand" plus "thousands of thousands" of angels around God's throne in heaven (the Greek text indicates that these numbers are plural, not singular). The Prophet Daniel saw a similar thing (Dan. 7:9-10). Multiplying 10,000 times one other 10,000 gives a total of 100,000,000. But John saw "ten thousand [plural] times ten thousand" [plural] plus thousands (plural) times thousands (plural), an indefinite number. Thus, there are hundreds and hundreds of millions, probably billions, of angels. It should be noted that the great host seen by Daniel and John consisted only of holy angels who serve God. It did not include all the fallen angels who follow and serve Satan.

Thus, the Bible confirms the existence of an enormous host of angels.

## The Nature of Angels: They are Spirit Beings

What kind of beings are angels? The Bible contains considerable revelation concerning their nature. First, angels are spirit beings by nature. The writer of Hebrews indicated that they are all "ministering spirits" (Heb. 1:14). Because angels are spirit beings, several things are true of them all.

**Angels Do Not Have Physical Bodies By Nature:** Jesus clearly stated that a spirit does not have flesh and bones, and He implied, therefore, that by nature a spirit cannot be touched or seen (Lk. 24:39). It follows, then, that because angels are spirit beings, it is not their nature to have physical bodies of flesh and bones.

The Apostle Paul indicated that the evil angels who fight against Christians are "spiritual" and, therefore, are not "flesh and blood" (Eph. 6:12).

Although angels do not have physical bodies by nature, there have been instances in which angels have temporarily taken on physical bodies that could be seen and touched when it was necessary. The Bible does not indicate how or from where they got those bodies, nor does it reveal what they did with the bodies when they were done with them. It simply records the fact that there have been such instances.

One such instance is found in Genesis 18-19. Three "men" appeared to Abraham on one occasion while he was living in the plains of Mamre (18:1-2). They had physical feet that could be washed with water (v. 4), and they ate food that Abraham had prepared for them (vv. 5-8). One of these "men" was the LORD (vv. 1, 13, 17, 20, 26, 33). While He talked with Abraham, the other two "men" went toward Sodom (vv. 16, 22).

The biblical account reveals that the two "men" who went to Sodom were "angels" (19:1, 15). In spite of this fact, Lot thought that they were men. He offered to wash their feet. When they stated that they would spend the night in the street, Lot pressured them strongly to stay in his house instead. In light of the sexual perversion for which Sodom was notorious, Lot knew that it would be a tragic mistake for two men to stay in the street during the night. After they went to Lot's house, they ate another meal (vv. 2-3).

It is apparent that the men of Sodom thought that the two visitors to their city were men. Later that night men of all ages came from the entire city, surrounded Lot's house, and demanded that he turn over the two "men" to them so that they could abuse them with their wicked practice. When Lot begged the men of Sodom not to make him turn over his two guests, they threatened to abuse him even worse and to break the door of his house in order to get at the two visitors (vv. 4-9).

In response to this threat, Lot's guests reached out their "hand," pulled Lot back into the house, and shut the door. From inside the house, separated by a door from the men of Sodom outside, they supernaturally inflicted blindness upon the Sodomites (vv. 10-11) without physically touching them. It is obvious that Lot's two visitors were not mere men.

The writer of Hebrews wrote, "Be not forgetful to entertain strangers; for thereby some have entertained angels unawares" (13:2). Surely he had in mind these instances in which two angels in physical bodies were shown hospitality by Abraham and Lot.

**Angels Do Not Have Sexuality By Nature:** It is not the nature of angels to have sexuality. This conclusion is based on two things. First, our sexuality is a very real part of our physical bodies, and sexual relationships involve physical body relationships — the two become one flesh (Mt. 19:4-6; 1 Cor. 6:13-20; 7:1-5). In light of this, because angels by nature do not have physical bodies, it should be evident that they do not by nature have sexuality.

Second, Jesus taught that when humans are resurrected from the dead, they will be like the angels in heaven in that they will neither marry nor be given in marriage (Mk. 12:25).

In His Matthew 19 teaching about marriage, Jesus indicated that God created humans "male and female" (with sexuality as part of their nature) and said, "For this cause [because I created humans with sexuality, here is how they are to use their sexuality] shall a man leave father and mother, and shall cleave [shall join himself sexually] to his wife, and they two shall be one flesh? Wherefore, they are no more two, but one flesh. What, therefore, God hath joined together, let not man put asunder" (vv. 4-6).[1] Through this teaching, Jesus indicated two things. First, God instituted marriage because He created humans with sexuality. In other words, marriage exists because of sexuality. Because marriage exists because of sexuality, it is inferred that if angels had sexuality by nature, marriage would exist among them. The fact that angels in heaven never marry strongly implies that they do not have sexuality by nature.

The second thing indicated by Jesus' teaching is that God created sexuality to be used in marriage. It would appear that because there is no marriage for angels in heaven, there is no reason for them to have sexuality.

**Angels Do Not Die:** Two things indicate that angels do not die. First, as noted earlier, angels do not have a physical body by nature. Humans die because they have physical bodies that are under a curse of sin (Gen. 2:17; 3:19; 5:3-5; Rom. 5:12; 6:23; 1 Cor. 15:56). Because angels do not have physical bodies, they do not experience physical death. Even the fallen angels, in spite of their sinful rebellion against God, do not die.

Second, Jesus taught that resurrected humans will be like angels in that they will not be able to die (Lk. 20:36). He thereby indicated that angels cannot die.

It can then be concluded that it is impossible to kill an angel. Later we shall see that holy and evil angels wage war against each other (Rev. 12:7). In this warfare, although they can inflict certain results on each other, no angel can kill another.

**Angels Are Invisible By Nature:** It is the nature of angels to be invisible to humans while humans are in their present mortal state. Two things prompt this conclusion. First, as noted earlier, Jesus implied that by nature a spirit cannot be touched or seen (Lk. 24:39). Because angels are spirits, it is their nature to be invisible to humans.

Second, the Apostle Paul indicated that in contrast with the things of earth that are visible, the thrones, dominions, principalities, and powers (terms for angels) in heaven are invisible (Col. 1:16).

According to the Scriptures, there are two exceptions to the rule of angels being invisible to mortal humans. First, on those occasions when angels have taken on physical bodies, they have been visible to mortal humans. An example of this is found in Genesis 18-19, where two angels appeared in physical bodies to Abraham and Lot.

The second exception is when God has given a special vision of angels to humans. A good example of this is found in 2 Kings 6:15-17. Syria waged war against Israel. The king of Syria, together with his military advisers, planned their strategy in secret. It appears that they purposely placed their forces in ambush along the routes where the king of Israel would travel.

Their goal was to capture him. However, each time they did this, the king of Israel did not travel that route, thereby frustrating the Syrian plans (vv. 8-10).

The king of Syria suspected that one of his advisers was a traitor. He demanded to know which one of them was revealing their secret plans to the king of Israel. One of the advisers insisted that none of them was a traitor. Instead, the king of Israel was learning their plans through an Israelite prophet, Elisha. The implication was that God listened to their secret planning sessions, revealed their plans to Elisha, and then Elisha informed the king of Israel (vv. 11-12).

The king of Syria sent a spy party into Israel to learn where Elisha was located. When he was told that the prophet was in the city of Dothan, the king sent a large force of soldiers, horses, and chariots to capture him. They surrounded the city at night (vv. 13-14).

The next morning Elisha's servant rose early, walked to the wall of the city, and looked out. He was not prepared for what he saw. The presence of the large Syrian military force around Dothan terrified him. He ran back to Elisha and blurted out, "Alas, my master! What shall we do?" (v. 15).

Elisha answered, "Fear not; for they who are with us are more than they who are with them" (v. 16). Elisha prayed and asked the LORD to open the servant's eyes to see what, by nature, could not be seen by his mortal eyes. God opened the servant's eyes, and he saw the mountain full of horses and chariots of fire around Elisha (v. 17). They were there to protect him. Over the years, students of the Bible have been convinced that what the servant saw was angels in the form of fiery horses and chariots. It appears that angels are capable of taking on any shape or form necessary to carry out a ministry. These particular angels were present and protecting Elisha before his servant saw them, but they were invisible to him until God gave him a special vision of them.

A similar incident happened in the 1950s during the MauMau

uprisings in Africa. As the result of MauMau threats, the missionaries and African Christians in a particular area moved to a central missionary compound. Sometime later they were forewarned that a large MauMau force intended to attack the compound and massacre its occupants on a certain night. The missionaries and African Christian men erected a barricade around the perimeter of the compound and positioned floodlights to illuminate the area outside the barricade. On the night of the anticipated attack, the men placed their wives and children in the most centralized building of the compound and asked them to pray. Then the men manned the barricade with whatever weapons were available. They waited all night, but the attack never came.

Sometime later one of the missionaries led one of the MauMau men to Christ. The man told the missionary that he had been part of a large MauMau force that surrounded the missionary compound on the night of the anticipated attack. He stated that they intended to overrun the compound and kill all of its occupants.

The missionary asked the new convert why the attack was not launched that night. He replied that just before their leader gave the order to attack, large fiery creatures suddenly appeared around the compound between them and the barricade. He stated that all the MauMaus saw them, and that none of them had seen anything like this before. The MauMaus were so terrified by the sudden appearance of these creatures that they ran away from the compound and were afraid to return.

Although the MauMaus saw the fiery creatures, none of the missionaries or African-Christian men saw them that night. After hearing the MauMau convert's account, the missionaries and African believers concluded that the fiery creatures were angels whom God had sent to protect His people. Thus, God gave a special vision of these angels to the MauMaus, but they were kept invisible to the Christians.[2]

**A Note Concerning Angelic Appearance:** In spite of the fact that angels do not by nature have sexuality, when they appeared in normal human form in Bible times (either with a tangible physical body as in Gen. 18-19 or in a vision as in Dan. 8:15; see 9:21), they always appeared as men. The Bible does not explain why this is so; it simply records what happened.

For example, the two angels who visited Lot in Sodom are called "men" (Gen. 19:5, 10, 12, 16). In addition, the men of Sodom viewed the two visitors as male, as indicated by their desire to commit sodomy with them (Gen. 19:4-7).

The angel Gabriel appeared to Daniel in the form of a man (Dan. 8:15; 9:21). The word translated "man" in 8:15 "specifically relates to a male at the height of his powers."[3] The word in 9:21 usually "denotes any individual male."[4]

Two angels appeared at Jesus' sepulcher in conjunction with His resurrection from the dead (Jn. 20:11-12). Luke indicated that they had the appearance of men (Lk. 24:4). The Greek word translated "men" is masculine in gender and refers to man specifically, "in contrast to woman."[5] Mark described one of these angels as "a young man" (Mk. 16:5). The Greek word translated "a young man" indicates that this angel appeared in the form of a man 24 to 40 years of age.[6] In addition, the pronoun in Mark 16:6, which is translated "he" and refers back to the angel of verse 5, is also masculine in gender.

The two angels who were seen at the time of Jesus' ascension appeared in the form of men (Acts 1:10). The word translated "men" is the same as that in Luke 24:4 which, as noted above, is masculine in gender and refers to a man in contrast to a woman. The pronoun in Acts 1:11, which is translated "Who" and refers back to the angels in verse 10, is also masculine in gender.

Zechariah 5:9 may seem to contradict the concept that when angels appeared in normal human form in Bible times, they always appeared as men. In this passage the prophet was shown a vision of two women with wings like a stork transporting by flight an ephod containing wickedness to the land of Shinar (Babylon).

There are reasons to doubt that these winged beings are angels. First, in every biblical account of angels appearing in normal human form there is no mention of wings being part of their appearance. (If the two angels who visited Lot in Sodom had appeared with wings, would the men of Sodom have regarded them as men?)

Second, the biblical passages that clearly refer to the wings of angels *never* compare their wings to those of a stork.

Third, the Bible refers to another woman who is given "two wings of a great eagle" (Rev. 12:14). In this instance, this winged woman is not an angel appearing in human form. The description of the woman given in Revelation 12:1-2, 4-5, when compared with Old Testament imagery (see Gen. 37:9-10; Isa. 54:5-6; Ezek. 16:7-14), reveals that she represents the nation of Israel through which the Messiah was born into the world.[7] The fact that this winged woman is not an angel indicates that the presence of winged women in the Bible does not require us to conclude that they are angels appearing in human form.

## The Nature of Angels:  They Are Created Beings

The second truth about the nature of angels is that they are creatures. They were created by God. They owe their existence to Him. They are not self-existing beings. This is indicated in several ways in the Bible. For example, in Psalm 148:2-4 all of God's angels and other parts of the universe are commanded to praise the LORD. Verse 5 explains why they should praise Him: "Let them praise the name of the LORD; for he commanded, and they were created." In addition, the Apostle Paul declared that angels were created (Col. 1:16).

Two major things should be noted concerning the creation of

angels:  the nature and time of their creation.

**The Nature of Their Creation:**  Because, as noted earlier, angels by nature do not have sexuality, they do not reproduce.  No angel has come into existence by reproduction.  By contrast, humans reproduce because they possess sexuality by nature.

Because angels do not reproduce, we must conclude that every angel was created *directly* and *individually* by God.  In line with this, in the Bible angels are called "sons of God" (Job 1:6; 2:1; 38:7), indicating that God is their source of origin, but they are never called "sons of angels."  By contrast, because humans are reproduced by humans, the Bible calls them "sons of men" (Eccl. 1:13; 2:3, 8; Dan. 5:21).

Because all angels were created directly and individually by God and do not reproduce, certain things must be true of them.  Angels have no ancestors, no offspring, and no families.  There are no mother, father, son, daughter, brother, sister, aunt, uncle, or cousin angels.  And although artistic representations of baby angels may be cute, there is no biblical verification to back up their existence.

By contrast, because humans reproduce, they have ancestors, offspring, blood relatives, and families.

In addition, because every angel was created directly and individually by God, they, contrary to popular opinion, are not departed spirits of deceased human beings.

Years ago a Christmas television special entitled "The Littlest Angel" portrayed the fictional story of a small boy who tried to catch a beautiful dove.  As the dove flew higher up the side of a mountain, the boy pursued it by climbing the mountain.  When he came to the peak and reached out to grasp the dove, the boy lost his footing and plunged to his death.  Immediately the boy's spirit ascended to heaven.  There adult angels were given the assignment of converting his spirit into an angel.  Through time, they accomplished their task, and so the boy's spirit became the littlest angel in heaven.

This was a sweet story, and it probably gave many people a warm, fuzzy feeling at Christmas, but it was contrary to reality. Departed spirits of deceased humans are not the source of angels. Each angel was created directly and individually by God.

**The Time of Their Creation:** The Bible does not give a clear, specific statement concerning when angels were created. However, the teaching of three passages, taken together, indicates the time of their creation.

The first passage is Job 38:6-7. It is important to note that it was God who spoke in this passage (see v. 1). He declared that when He created the earth, "the morning stars sang together, and all the sons of God shouted for joy" (v. 7). God thereby revealed that the morning stars/sons of God were already present to observe His act of bringing the earth into existence, and they were so impressed with this great work that they sang and shouted His praises. This declaration of God indicates that the morning stars/sons of God existed before the earth was created.

Who were these morning stars/sons of God? In attempting to identify them, we should note three things. First, the fact that they sang and shouted God's praises indicates that the morning stars/sons of God were personal beings, not impersonal objects.

Second, the Book of Job is an Old Testament poetic book. A major characteristic of ancient Hebrew poetry was parallelism, where two lines express the same thought but through different words. The two lines "the morning stars sang together" and "all the sons of God shouted for joy" of Job 38:7 are an example of Hebrew parallelism; therefore, they express the same thought and do not represent two sets of beings.

Third, "the sons of God" were mentioned earlier in the Book of Job (1:6; 2:1). Scholars are convinced that in those passages and Job 38:7 "the sons of God" are angels. This means, then, following the poetic use of parallelism, that the expression "the morning stars" is also a reference to angels.

In light of what has been seen, it can be concluded that in Job 38:6-7 God revealed that the angels were already existing and present when He created the earth.

The second passage related to the issue of when angels were created is Exodus 20:11. There Moses declared that "in six days the LORD made heaven and earth, the sea, and all that in them is, and rested the seventh day." (The Hebrew text says "the heavens" [plural] "and the earth.") This statement is very significant because it indicates that within the scope of the six days of creation of Genesis 1 God created not only the heavens and the earth, but also *all the different kinds of life forms that exist in the heavens, the earth, and the sea* (see Gen. 2:1-4; Neh. 9:6).

The Bible indicates that the angels are a kind of life form that exists in the heavenly realm (1 Ki. 22:19; Ps. 103:19-21; Mt. 18:10; 22:30; 24:36; Lk. 2:13-15). As a result, Moses' declaration in Exodus 20:11 is applicable to them. It strongly implies that the angels were created within the scope of the six days of creation of Genesis 1, not before or after those days.

The third passage that sheds light on the time when angels were created is Genesis 1:1 which states, "In the beginning God created the heaven and the earth" (the Hebrew text says "the heavens" [plural] "and the earth," exactly as does Exodus 20:11). Because Exodus 20:11 indicated that the heavens and the earth were created within the scope of the six days of creation of Genesis 1, it can be concluded that the creative activity of Genesis 1:1 took place within the scope of those same six days, not before or after those days.

In light of this, a reading of Genesis 1:1-5 prompts the further conclusion that those verses refer to the *first* day of the *six* days of creation.

In light of these passages, three strong conclusions can be made about the time the angels were created. First, they were created sometime before the creation of the earth (Job 38:6-7).

Second, they were created within the scope of the six days of creation of Genesis 1, not before or after those days (Ex. 20:11). Third, God created the heavens and the earth on the first day of the six days of creation (Gen. 1:1).

Thus, the angels were created by God on the first day of the six days of creation, but before the earth was created on that same day. It is interesting to note the order of Moses' statement in Genesis 1:1. He referred to the heavens first, then the earth. It would appear that early on the first day God created the heavens. Later on that day He created the angels to inhabit the heavens. Still later on the first day He created the earth in its undeveloped, uninhabited state.

## The Nature of Angels:  They Are Personal Beings

The Bible indicates that three different kinds of personal beings exist in the universe:    divine, angelic, and human. Although the beings in each of these kinds possess some attributes that differ from those in the other two kinds, all possess the three attributes of personality:  intellect, emotions, and will.

**Angels and the Attributes of Personality:**  The Bible presents evidences to the effect that angels possess the attributes of personality.

**Intellect**:  Angels, other divine and human beings possess an intellect that is far superior to that of animals.  According to 2 Samuel 14:20 the holy angels possess great wisdom.  In addition, they have the ability to communicate intelligent thoughts by arranging words in logical order to form propositional statements (Gen. 19:1-2; Mt. 1:20-21; 2:13, 19-20; Lk. 1:11-20, 26-38).

When Jesus confronted a demon-possessed man in the synagogue at Capernaum, the demon used intelligent language to speak to the Lord and possessed knowledge, discernment, and the ability to understand a verbal command (Lk. 4:33-35).  From all we can determine, demons are fallen, evil angels.

Although angels possess a great degree of intelligence, they do not know everything. They do not know the day and hour of Christ's Second Coming (Mt. 24:36). They learn about the manifold wisdom of God by watching the way He builds the church (Eph. 3:10). God's work of saving sinful human beings is a mystery to them (1 Pet. 1:9-12).

**Emotions**: Angels possess and experience emotions. When they watched God create the earth, they experienced great joy (Job 38:4-7). As an angel, Satan will experience great wrath when he and his fallen angels are cast to the earth from their heavenly sphere during the future Tribulation (Rev. 12:7-12).

**Will**: The Apostle Paul referred to people who are taken captive by Satan "at his will" (2 Tim. 2:26). He thereby indicated that Satan, who is an angel, has a will. Early in history, some angels decided to rebel against God and thereby became evil. Other angels chose to remain loyal to God and thereby remained holy. The fact that angels made such decisions indicates that they have a will. They are not simply driven to serve God.

In light of these evidences, we can conclude that all angels possess the attributes of personality and, therefore, are personal beings.

## The Nature of Angels: They Are Powerful Beings

Angels possess great power. David wrote, "Bless the LORD, ye his angels, that excel in strength" (Ps. 103:20). The Apostle Paul ascribed the term "power" or "powers" to angels (Eph. 2:2; 3:10; 6:12; Col. 1:16), and he declared that they are "mighty" (2 Th. 1:7). Peter indicated that angels have great "power and might" (2 Pet. 2:11). The Apostle John described angels as being "strong" (Rev. 5:2) and "mighty" (Rev. 10:1; 18:21) and "having great power" (Rev. 18:1).

The Bible presents demonstrations of their great power. For example, angels had the power to inflict blindness upon the men of Sodom without the use of physical means (Gen. 19:10-11). An angel shut the mouths of lions so that they could not hurt Daniel (Dan. 6:22). Because of unbelief, Zecharias, the father of John the Baptist, was inflicted with the inability to speak for a period of time by the angel Gabriel (Lk. 1:19-22). The mere presence of an angel caused a great earthquake (Mt. 28:2). An angel freed apostles from imprisonment by causing chains to fall off and prison doors to open without using keys or physical force (Acts 5:17-19; 12:1-11). An angel smote King Herod Agrippa I with a fatal illness because he accepted the ascription of deity to himself by some of his subjects (Acts 12:20-23). During the future Tribulation, angels will inflict awesome judgments upon the world (Rev. 8-18). At the Second Coming of Christ, angels will remove all living unsaved people from the earth and will cast them into a terrible place of judgment (Mt. 13:37-42, 47-50). At that same coming, the remnant of saved Jews alive on the earth will be gathered from the whole world to their homeland by angels (Mt. 24:29-31; cp. Isa. 27:12-13).

The Bible reveals that the power of angels is superior to the power of human beings. The Apostle Peter indicated that angels "are greater in power and might" than mortal people (2 Pet. 2:11). Paul commanded Christians to "be strong in the Lord, and in the power of his might" and to "Put on the whole armor of God" in order to stand against attacks by evil angels (Eph. 6:10-18). He thereby implied that, by themselves, mortal Christians are no match for the power of evil angels. The only way they can deal effectively with that superior angelic power is to use the equipment God has made available to believers. It is therefore clear that there is a major distinction between the power of angels and the power of human beings. Angelic power could be classified as *supernatural*. By contrast, human power is only *natural*.

It is important to note that although angelic power is supernatural, it has limitations. Angels are not omnipotent. The Bible indicates that only deity is all-powerful and, therefore, angels are no match for the power possessed by the persons of the triune Godhead. The reality of this has been demonstrated in several ways. God had the power to imprison a group of angels in a place of darkness and to keep them there until their final future judgment (2 Pet. 2:4; Jude 6). He also had the power to restrict Satan's attacks against Job (Job 1:8-12; 2:1-6). Christ had the power to cast out demons (fallen angels) and to make them go wherever He commanded (Mt. 9:32-33; Lk. 8:26-36).

At the end of the present earth's history, God will crush a final satanic revolt and cast Satan into the lake of fire, where he will be constantly tormented for all eternity (Rev. 20:7-10; cp. Mt. 25:41). This is most significant because it appears that in his original holy state, Satan was the most powerful angel created by God (Ezek. 28:11-15). Because the most powerful angel is no match for God's power, it is certain that no angel possesses power equal to God's.

## ENDNOTES

[1] The word translated "cleave" in Mt. 19:5 refers to sexual union. See K.L. Schmidt, "Kollao, proskollao," *Theological Dictionary of the New Testament*, ed. Gerhard Kittel, trans. and ed. Geoffrey W. Bromiley, III (Grand Rapids: Wm. B. Eerdmans Publishing Company, 1965), pp. 822-23.

[2] The author heard this account related in the 1950s by a fellow schoolmate in Bible school. She was the daughter of missionaries who experienced this incident.

[3] John N. Oswalt, "geber," *Theological Wordbook of the Old Testament*, Vol. I, ed. by R. Laird Harris, Gleason L. Archer, Jr., and Bruce K. Waltke (Chicago: Moody Press, 1980), p. 148.

[4] Thomas E. McComiskey, "ish," *Theological Wordbook of the Old Testament*, Vol. I, p. 38.

[5] William F. Arndt and F. Wilbur Gingrich, *A Greek-English Lexicon of the New Testament*, 4th rev. ed. (Chicago: The

University of Chicago Press, 1957), p. 65.

[6] *Ibid.*, p. 536.

[7] For further treatment of this identification see: Renald E. Showers, *MARANATHA: Our Lord, Come!* (Bellmawr, NJ: The Friends of Israel Gospel Ministry, 1995), p. 44.

## 2

# THE COUNCIL, RANKS, AND DESIGNATIONS OF ANGELS

## The Council of Angels

Psalm 89 refers to "the congregation of the saints" and "the assembly of the saints" (vv. 5, 7). Because the Psalms consist of Hebrew poetry that is characterized by parallelism, these two expressions refer to the same group.

The Hebrew word translated "assembly" also meant "counsel" or "council." Its primary meaning was "confidential speech," but its meaning was extended to refer to "a circle of trusted intimates" to whom a person speaks in confidence.[1]

The Hebrew word translated "the saints" literally means "holy ones." Joseph Addison Alexander stated that this word "is entirely different from that usually rendered *saints*. The latter is always applied to men, the former usually to superior beings, *i.e.* angels."[2] He thereby indicated that the congregation or assembly of the saints in Psalm 89:5-7 consists of holy angels, not human beings.

Other Old Testament scholars agree that the word translated "the saints" is a reference to angels. Franz Delitzsch asserted that in Psalm 89:5-7, God's way of acting "is praised in the assembly of the holy ones, *i.e.* of the spirits in the other world, the angels, for He is peerlessly exalted above the heavens and the angels."[3]

Three other things in the biblical text indicate that it is referring to angels. First, the Hebrew language of verses 5 and 6 indicate that this assembly of holy ones is located in the heavens. Alexander wrote, "The parallelism of *heavens* and *holy ones* shews that the former are here put for their inhabitants."[4] In other words, the Hebrew parallelism uses "the heavens" that praise God as a synonym of the holy ones who dwell in the heavenly realm. Thus, the heavens praise God through the holy ones who dwell in the heavens praising Him.

Second, the Hebrew expression in verse 6 that refers to the holy ones and is translated "the sons of the mighty" has the literal meaning "sons of God."[5] The Hebrew parallelism of verse 6 indicates that these sons of God are in the heavenly realm. In the earlier study of Job 38:7, it was noted that the expression "sons of God" is used for angels. Concerning this expression as it is used in Psalm 89:6, Delitzsch asserted that it refers not to "the mighty of the earth," but to angels.[6]

Third, the Hebrew parallelism of verse 7 indicates that the holy ones are located "about" God. The word translated "about" means to "encircle" or "surround."[7] Thus, these holy ones surround or encircle the unique presence of God in His heaven.

When the Apostle John was given revelation concerning God's heaven and throne (Rev. 4:1-2), he saw 24 elders and four living beings around God's throne (vv. 4, 6), "heard the voice of many angels round about the throne" praising God and Christ (Rev.

5:11-13), and saw "all the angels" standing "round about the throne" worshiping and praising God (Rev. 7:11-12; see Neh. 9:6; Ps. 103:19-21). In light of what John observed and the fact that the holy ones of Psalm 89:5-7 also surround God in heaven and praise and reverence Him, we can conclude that they too are angels. In line with this conclusion, Alexander wrote, *"Those about him, i.e.* those immediately surrounding him, his heavenly attendants, the angels."[8]

On the basis of all that has been noted concerning Psalm 89:5-7, the following conclusion can be drawn: The holy angels in God's heaven surround His unique presence and throne and constitute a great council of trusted intimates to whom God reveals His confidential plans and purposes. Commenting on verse 7, Alexander stated, "The angels are again called *holy ones*, but furthermore described as the privy council, the confidential intimates, of God himself."[9] What a great privilege is theirs! It is no wonder, then, that holy angels were able to deliver knowledge of some of God's plans and purposes to human beings during Bible times.

The Psalm 89 passage also indicates that these holy angels acknowledge that God is unique and that not even they can be compared to Him.

## Ranks and Designations of Angels

It appears that God created angels with different degrees of intelligence and power, established various ranks of angels on the basis of these differences, and organized them according to rank similar to the way armed forces are organized. One indication of this is the fact that God is called "LORD of hosts" numerous times in the Old Testament. The Hebrew word translated "hosts" means "armies"; thus, God is "LORD of armies."[10]

The Bible indicates that the holy angels constitute a powerful heavenly army or armies that carry out God's commands (1 Ki. 22:19; Ps. 103:20-21), serve as His chariots (Ps. 68:17), and are divided into legions (Mt. 26:53). In light of this, God's title "LORD of armies" indicates that He is the Commander in Chief of the angelic armies of heaven.

Another indication of holy angels arranged according to rank as an army is the fact that some angels are under the command of other angels. For example, the angel Michael has angels under his command for the purpose of waging angelic warfare (Rev. 12:7).

As we examine the biblical terms applied to angels, please keep in mind that in some instances it is difficult to determine whether a term refers to a rank or is simply a designation not related to rank.

**Cherubim**: The fullest description of cherubim is given in Ezekiel 1:5-24 and 10:1-22. The four cherubim described there were part human and part animal in appearance. They each had a body and hands similar to a man's (1:5, 8), but each had four faces pointing in four directions (faces of a man, a lion, an ox, and an eagle; 1:6, 10) and four wings (1:6, 11). Their feet were like those of a calf (1:7). They had the gleaming appearance of polished bronze, burning coals of fire, or flaming torches (1:7, 13). Their entire bodies, backs, hands, and wings were full of eyes (10:12). They could move very quickly in any direction (1:19-21). When they moved, their wings made a very loud noise (1:24).

Apparently the cherubim constitute the highest rank of angels. Two things prompt this conclusion. First, of all the angels, they seem to have the closest relationship to God. Second, the Bible refers to them more than to any other rank of angels.

After God drove Adam and Eve from the Garden of Eden, He placed cherubim as guards at the east of the garden (Gen. 3:24).

A major part of God's moving chariot-throne consists of the four cherubim described above (Ezek. 1:5-28; 10:1-22; 11:22). In line with this, the mercy seat of the ark of the covenant, over which God dwelt in a unique sense, is called "the chariot of the cherubim" (1 Chr. 28:18).

Two cherubim were fashioned from gold for the ends of the mercy seat on top of the ark of the covenant in the Holy of Holies of the Tabernacle and Solomon's Temple (Ex. 25:17-22). God dwelt in a unique sense between those cherubim above the mercy seat (Num. 7:89; 2 Ki. 19:15; Ps. 80:1). Because God intended the earthly Tabernacle and Temple to be "the example and shadow of heavenly things" (Heb. 8:5), we can conclude that in His heaven God dwells in the midst of cherubim as He sits upon His throne.

Visual representations of cherubim were used extensively in the Tabernacle and Solomon's Temple. In addition to the cherubim on the ends of the mercy seat, figures of cherubim were woven into the ten curtains of the Tabernacle and into the veil that separated its Holy of Holies from the Holy Place (Ex. 26:1, 31).

Two large cherubim (approximately 15 feet tall with each wing somewhat longer than seven feet) made of olive wood and overlaid with gold were placed in the Holy of Holies of Solomon's Temple (1 Ki. 6:23-28). These figures completely overshadowed the ark of the covenant, which was placed between them (1 Ki. 8:6-7).

Solomon had figures of cherubim carved into all the walls and doors of the Temple (1 Ki. 6:29-35) and placed on the borders and plates of the ten brass bases of the portable lavers (1 Ki. 7:29-38). He also had cherubim woven into the veil that separated the Temple's Holy of Holies from its Holy Place (2 Chr. 3:14).

The future millennial Temple will have figures of cherubim carved into all of its walls and doors (Ezek. 41:18-25).

Apparently not all cherubim have identically the same appearance as the four who are part of God's chariot-throne. The millennial Temple will portray cherubim with only two faces (the faces of a man and a young lion; Ezek. 41:18-19). This may indicate that there are several different orders within the rank of cherubim.

**Seraphim:** Isaiah 6:1-7 is the only place in the Bible where the designation "seraphim" is applied to angels. Perhaps this is the only biblical revelation concerning this group of angels.

The seraphim have faces, feet, and hands, and each one has six wings (vv. 2, 6). Two wings cover the face, two cover the feet (probably as expressions of humility and reverence in the presence of God),[11] and two are used for flying (v. 2).

The location and activity of the seraphim are significant. Isaiah saw them standing above the throne of God (vv. 1-2); therefore, they were covering the unique presence of God and His throne. Originally this responsibility of covering belonged to the exalted holy angel whom God addressed as "the anointed cherub that covereth" and "covering cherub" (Ezek. 28:14, 16). Eventually this exalted angel became very proud because of his magnificent nature and, as a result, rebelled against God (Ezek. 28:12, 15, 17).

In his rebellion, this exalted angel boasted that he would make himself "like the Most High" (Isa. 14:14). Because God was the ultimate sovereign of the whole universe, even the Commander in Chief over the angelic armies of heaven, this rebellious cherub asserted that he would make himself that ultimate sovereign. In essence he was saying, "God, you're not unique, one-of-a-kind. I can make myself just like you." Because God's uniqueness is the essence of His holiness (Ex. 15:11; 1 Sam. 2:2; Isa. 40:18, 25),[12] this assertion was an attack on the holiness of God. Because of this attack, God cast this rebellious cherub out of His heaven (Ezek. 28:16) and changed the cherub's name to Satan (lit. "Adversary"[13]) because he had become the great enemy of God.

Isaiah 6 makes it apparent that God replaced the rebellious cherub with the seraphim. They now stand where he stood over the unique presence of God and His throne in heaven, and they carry out the responsibility of covering that he once held. He attacked the uniqueness or holiness of God, but they do the opposite. They cry out, "Holy, holy, holy, is the LORD of hosts" (Isa. 6:3) and thereby assert that God is unique, the ultimate sovereign of the whole universe, even the Commander in Chief over the angelic armies of heaven.

The word "seraphim" comes from a root word that means "burn."[14]   As a result, the word "seraphim" means "burning ones."  It may be that this designation has been given to these angels because of their appearance, but also because, in contrast to the rebellious anointed cherub, they burn with zeal for God and His holiness.

Do the seraphim constitute a rank of angels separate from that of the cherubim?  Because they differ in appearance, location, and function from the four cherubim who are part of God's chariot-throne, it may be that they do.  Many Bible scholars are convinced of this.  However, in light of two other facts, it may be that they are another form and order of the cherubim.

First, as noted earlier, apparently not all cherubim have identically the same appearance as the four who are part of God's chariot-throne.

Second, the seraphim cover the unique presence of God and His throne in heaven.  The golden cherubim of the mercy seat of the ark of the covenant and the large figures of cherubim between which the ark of the covenant sat in Solomon's Temple also covered the unique presence of God and His seat on earth with their wings (Ex. 25:17-22; 1 Ki. 6:23-28; 8:6-7).  Because, as noted earlier, God intended the earthly Tabernacle and Temple to be an example and shadow of what is in heaven, it would appear that He intended them to indicate that cherubim cover His unique presence and throne in heaven.  Because the earthly Tabernacle and Temple were constructed long after Satan was evicted from his covering position and replaced by the seraphim, it would appear that God intended them to indicate that cherubim cover His unique presence and throne in heaven ever since He replaced the rebellious cherub with the seraphim.  It may be, then, that the seraphim are the cherubim who now have the covering responsibility.

**The Four Living Beings**: In Revelation 4:6-9, the Apostle John saw "four living creatures" in the middle of and around the throne of God in heaven.

In appearance, the first living being was similar to a lion, the second to a calf, the third had a face like that of a man, and the fourth was similar to a flying eagle (v. 7). Each living being had six wings (v. 8), and the entire body of each was full of eyes (vv. 6, 8).

The primary function of these four living beings at all periods of day and night is to exalt God. They continually declare His holiness (uniqueness), omnipotence, and eternality (v. 8). This is not their only function, however. It appears that in addition to their personal worship of God, they serve as worship leaders in heaven. Each time they give glory, honor, and thanks to God, they prompt the 24 elders to fall down before God, worship Him, and cast their crowns before Him (vv. 9-11).

The four living beings will be involved with significant future events. When Christ takes the sealed scroll from the hand of God before the beginning of the future Tribulation, the four living beings and the 24 elders will fall down before Him. They will worship Him by singing a new song honoring Christ as the only one worthy to take the scroll and break its seals because He has redeemed human beings and made them kings and priests (Rev. 5:7-10).

This worship of Christ by the four living beings and the 24 elders will prompt the great host of angels in heaven to worship Him (5:11-12) and then every creature in the entire universe to worship God and Christ (5:13).

At the conclusion of all of this worship, the four living beings will express their hearty approval of it. This will prompt the 24 elders to fall down before God and worship Him (5:14).

As each of the first four seals of the sealed scroll are broken by Christ during the first half of the future Tribulation, one of the four living beings will command the horse and rider of each seal to come forth to administer their form of God's wrath upon the world (Rev. 6:1-7).

The four living beings will be present to witness the great host of angels in heaven falling before God and worshiping Him in response to the worship of God and Christ by the great multitude of Tribulation saints who will come out of the Great Tribulation to heaven through death (Rev. 7:9-15). They also will be present to hear a new song in heaven, a song that only the unique group of 144,000 Jewish men of the future Tribulation (see Rev. 7:1-8) will be able to learn (Rev. 14:1-5).

In the latter part of the future Tribulation, one of the four living beings will give seven angels seven golden vials or bowls containing the seven last plagues, which will complete the pouring out of God's Tribulation-period wrath (Rev. 15:1, 7).

The four living beings and the 24 elders will fall down before God and worship Him because of His destruction of the great harlot, the future Babylon, in conjunction with the pouring out of the seventh bowl judgment (Rev. 19:1-4).

In light of all these activities, it is evident that the four living beings play a key role in the worship of God and Christ, and they will have a significant relationship to the administration of some of God's future Tribulation judgments of the world.

Who are these four living beings? There are reasons to conclude that they are angels. First, their location in heaven indicates that they stand closest to the unique presence of God and His throne. They immediately surround Him and His throne. Because the ark of the covenant, which God intended to be an example and shadow of what is in heaven, portrayed angelic cherubim standing closest to the unique presence of God and His seat, God must have intended it to communicate that the beings who stand closest to His presence and throne in heaven are also angels.

Second, the four living beings have features in common with

both the cherubim and seraphim. The four living beings of Revelation and the cherubim of Ezekiel both are described as living beings and are four in number (Rev. 4:6; Ezek. 1:5). Both groups have appearances associated with a lion, a calf, a man, and an eagle, although those associations are not identical (Rev. 4:7; Ezek. 1:6, 10). The bodies of both are covered with eyes (Rev. 4:6, 8; Ezek. 10:12).

Each of the four living beings of Revelation and each of the seraphim of Isaiah 6 have six wings (Rev. 4:8; Isa. 6:2). In addition, both the four living beings and the seraphim emphasize and announce the holiness or uniqueness of God (Rev. 4:8; Isa. 6:3).

Because the four living beings have these features in common with the cherubim and seraphim, and because the cherubim and seraphim are angels, it seems an obvious conclusion that the four living beings are a type of angel.

It may be that the four living beings of Revelation are cherubim of a different form and order from those in Ezekiel. This is possible in light of the features in common with the cherubim of Ezekiel and the seraphim of Isaiah. Also, the earlier observations that apparently not all cherubim are identical, that the seraphim may be cherubim of a different form and order from those in Ezekiel, and that the four living beings of Revelation and the cherubim of the ark of the covenant were located closest to the unique presence of God point to this possibility.

**Archangel**: The term "archangel" appears only twice in the Bible (1 Th. 4:16; Jude 9). It means "chief messenger" or "ruling messenger."

First Thessalonians 4:16 refers to an archangel who, with a loud voice, will announce the coming of Christ to rapture the church out of the world.

Only one archangel, Michael, is actually named in the Bible (Jude 9). In ancient times Michael contended with Satan about the body of Moses. Near the middle of the future Tribulation,

Michael and the holy angels under his authority will wage war in the heavenly realm against Satan and the evil angels under his authority. Michael and his angels will cast Satan and his angels out of their heaven to the earth (Rev. 12:7-9).

Michael serves as the guardian angelic prince of the nation of Israel (Dan. 10:21; 12:1). In light of this, when, in the middle of the future Tribulation, Satan and his Antichrist begin to attack Israel with a vengeance, Michael will have to go into all-out action to prevent the total annihilation of the nation (Rev. 12:13-17; Dan 9:27; 12:1). All of these things indicate that Michael is truly a ruling angel with other holy angels under his authority.

Although the angel Gabriel is not called an archangel in the Bible, many scholars believe that he is one.[15] It does appear that he was a chief messenger of God because he delivered several very important messages from God to human beings. He communicated crucial information concerning the future of Israel and the Messiah to Daniel (Dan. 8:15-27; 9:21-27). He informed Zacharias the priest that he would be the father of John the Baptist, the forerunner of the Messiah (Lk. 1:5-20). He revealed to the virgin Mary that she would give birth to the Messiah (Lk. 1:26-38).

It is interesting to note that rabbinical statements in the Jewish Talmud teach that God created four archangels to be the heads over all other angels and to surround His throne. According to this tradition, the names of the four archangels are Michael, Gabriel, Uriel and Raphael.[16] The names Uriel and Raphael, however, are not applied to any angels in the inspired books of the Bible.

**Princes**: This designation refers to powerful angels, both holy and evil, who are assigned by God or Satan to positions of authority over nations to influence their decisions and actions (Dan. 10:13, 20, 21; 12:1). God has assigned the archangel Michael to the position of prince over Israel (Dan. 10:21; 12:1). These holy and evil angelic princes wage war against each other in relationship to the affairs of nations.

The designation of "prince" is given to Satan as well, referring to his position of authority over the evil angels (Mt. 9:34; Eph. 2:2) and the world system (Jn. 12:31; 14:30; 16:11).

**Angels**: This term simply means "messenger."[17] It refers to a being who is sent by another with a commission.[18] Both God and Satan send forth angels with assignments.

Although the term "angels" is used in a general sense to refer to all ranks of angels (Mt. 24:36; 25:31; Heb. 1:6), it seems that it also is used in a specific sense to refer to angels of the lowest rank (Rom. 8:38; 1 Pet. 3:22, where angels are mentioned in a group separate from higher angelic authorities).

**Sons of God, sons of the mighty**: These designations (Job 1:6; 38:7; Ps. 89:6) indicate two things concerning angels. First, their source is God. He created them. Second, God created them after His likeness.[19]

**Mighty ones**: This designation emphasizes the supernatural power possessed by angels (Joel 3:11; cp. Ps. 103:20).

**Watchers**: This term used for angels in Daniel 4:13, 17, and 23 meant "waking, watchful."[20] Because angels do not have physical bodies, they have no need of sleep. As a result, these angels are able to labor untiringly day and night, watching over the affairs of God, making sure that His commands are put into effect. Concerning these angels, Gleason L. Archer, Jr. wrote, "From v. 17 we infer that this particular class of angels (if a special class is intended) has some involvement with executing the judgmental decrees of God, including their official pronouncement to mankind."[21]

**Holy ones; elect angels**: These designations (Dan. 4:13, 17; 1 Tim. 5:21; cp. Mk. 8:38) refer to the good angels—those who never rebelled against God. It emphasizes their inner nature. They are sinless beings without the inclination to sin.

God created all the angels as sinless beings (Gen. 1:31), but in their original state they were not confirmed or locked into sin-lessness. The only way they could become confirmed in sinless-ness was if they of their own volition chose to remain loyal to God. If they chose to rebel against God, they would lose their sinlessness and be confirmed or locked into evil.

As noted earlier, the anointed cherub (who is now called "Satan") chose to rebel against God (Ezek. 28:14-15). He want-ed to be "like the Most High" (Isa. 14:14); therefore, because God had angels under His dominion, Satan felt compelled to have the same. But because he was only a creature and not the Creator, he lacked the ability to create other angels. The most he could hope for was to persuade God's angels to join him in his rebellion against God.

Satan succeeded in convincing a significant amount of God's angels to join him, as evidenced by the biblical reference to Satan and "his angels" (Rev. 12:7-9; Mt. 25:41). Those angels who chose to rebel against God thereby confirmed or locked them-selves into evil forever. Those who chose to remain loyal to God when confronted with Satan's proposal thereby confirmed them-selves in sinlessness. It is they who are called "the holy ones" and "the elect angels."

**Principalities, might, powers, dominions, rulers of the darkness of this world, spiritual wickedness in high places, authorities, rule, thrones**: These designations are the transla-tions of seven different Greek terms in the following passages of the New Testament: Romans 8:38; 1 Corinthians 15:24; Ephesians 1:21; 2:2; 3:10; 6:12; Colossians 1:16; 2:10, 15; 1 Peter 3:22. It is difficult to determine two things concerning the seven Greek terms. First, do they refer to seven different ranks of angels? Many scholars are convinced that at least some of the terms refer to different classes,[22] but not necessarily to seven. F. F. Bruce wrote,

In all, five classes of angel-princes seem to be distinguished in the NT—thrones, principalities, authorities, powers and dominions. They probably represent the highest orders of the angelic realm, but the variety of ways in which the titles are combined in the NT warns us against the attempt to reconstruct a fixed hierarchy from them.[23]

Second, what are the distinctions between these different classes? All seven Greek terms indicate beings who have the power to exercise authority, but they do not define the various levels of power or spheres of authority that may distinguish these classes.

Perhaps the term that comes closest to defining the level of power or sphere of authority for the angels in its class is the one translated "the rulers of the darkness of this world" in Ephesians 6:12. That term means "world-ruler,"[24] and refers to a being "who aspires to world control."[25]    E. K. Simpson indicated that in Ephesians 6:12 it identifies "unseen spiritual potentates who make human despots and false systems of thought their tools of dominion."[26]  In other words, in that passage it refers to invisible, powerful, evil angels who influence and control powerful human rulers and movements for evil on earth. It may very well be the term for the evil angels who, as noted earlier, are assigned by Satan to nations with the designation of "prince" (Dan. 10:13, 20-21; 12:1).

Such passages as Colossians 1:16 and John 1:3 clearly indicate that the angels who belong to all of these classes of powerful authority were created by Christ. This means that all angels were originally holy.  Other passages, such as Ephesians 6:12 and Colossians 2:15, make it obvious that some of those angels are now evil. They are those angels who chose to rebel against God. As a result of this rebellion by some angels, today the classes of powerful ruling spirits are divided between holy and evil angels.[27]

**Morning stars:** As noted earlier, God declared that the angels, as morning stars, sang His praises when they observed Him create the earth on the first day of creation. Why did God call the

angels "morning stars"? The Bible does not explain the significance of this designation, so the most we can do is conjecture.
There is more than one possible explanation.

First, the Greek word translated "morning" in the expression
"morning star" in Revelation 2:28 means "early."[28]  In light of
this, perhaps the angels are called "morning stars" because God
brought them into existence very early, even before the earth,
when He created the universe.

Second, the heavenly body that historically has been called
"the morning star" is very bright—so bright that it is still visible
in the light of the dawn. It may be that God called the angels
"morning stars" to emphasize the brightness of their appearance
(see Ezek. 1:7, 13-14; Mt. 28:2-3; Acts 10:3, 30; 12:7).

**Twenty-four elders**: Many sincere students of the Bible disagree concerning the identification of the 24 elders whom John
saw in heaven (Rev. 4:4). Some assert that they are 24 men who
serve in heaven as representatives of Israel, or the church, or a
combination of Israel and the church. This position has good supporting arguments. The strongest is the fact that some Greek
texts and English translations have the 24 elders claiming that
Christ has redeemed them by His blood "out of every kindred,
and tongue, and people, and nation," that He has made them kings
and priests unto God, and that they will reign on the earth (Rev.
5:8-10). Because, as shall be seen later, God does not redeem
angels, and because it is human saints who will reign on the earth
during the Millennium (Dan. 7:18, 22, 27; Rev. 20:4), these
claims argue strongly in favor of the 24 elders being human
beings, not angels.

Other students believe that the 24 elders are angels. One student even went so far as to say that the 24 elders of Revelation
"are certainly to be regarded as angelic powers."[29]  Those who
take this position also have supporting arguments.

First, some argue that the most reliable Greek manuscript of

Revelation indicates that the claims of Revelation 5:8-10 are applied by the 24 elders, not to themselves, but to another class of beings. According to this text, the elders are not part of the group of beings who have been redeemed, made kings and priests, and who will reign on the earth.[30] In other words, they could be something other than human beings.

Second, it should be noted that the claims of Revelation 5:8-10 are not made exclusively by the 24 elders. The four living beings, who, as noted earlier, are angels, make the same claims together with the elders. Because they can make the same claims without being humans, we are not required to conclude that the 24 elders are humans just on the basis of those claims.[31]

Third, Revelation passages present redeemed human beings and the 24 elders as separate, distinct groups (7:9-17; 11:16-18; 14:1-5).[32]

Fourth, the 24 elders and their thrones are located *around* the throne of God (Rev. 4:4). By contrast Revelation portrays redeemed human beings in heaven either *under* an altar (6:9) or *before* the throne of God (7:9, 15).

Fifth, the 24 elders are *seated* in the unique presence of God in heaven (Rev. 4:4; 11:16). In the ancient world and in the Bible, the act of sitting was often used as "a mark of particular distinction."[33] For example, rulers sat on their thrones while their subjects *stood* before them. This distinguished the ruler from his subjects (Ex. 11:5). Normally the only subjects who were given the privilege of sitting in the presence of a king were his special favorites (Neh. 2:6).[34] The fact that God, who sits forever as King of the universe (Ps. 29:10; 47:7-8; 99:1; Isa. 6:1, 5), grants the 24 elders the privilege of sitting in His presence indicates that they have a special relationship with Him. By contrast, in Revelation redeemed human beings do not sit in the presence of God the King (6:9-11; 7:9-15; 15:2-4).

Sixth, the 24 elders are seated on thrones (Rev. 4:4). In the Bible thrones serve as "a symbol of government (2 S. 3:10; cf.

also Is. 14:13)."[35]  It would appear that "the thrones of the 24 elders in 4:4 are the seats of powers which bear rule in heaven."[36] The fact that the elders praise and reverence God by falling down before Him and casting their crowns before His throne indicates that whatever their sphere of ruling authority may be, they exercise that authority in subjection to Him (Rev. 4:10-11).[37] Through these acts of worship, they acknowledge that He is superior to them and that they cannot be compared to Him.

The 24 elders are the only creatures of God portrayed as sitting on thrones in heaven *before* the events of the Tribulation and Second Coming of Christ. The redeemed human beings are not portrayed in this manner. They will not be seated on thrones until Christ returns to earth in His Second Coming for His millennial reign (Mt. 19:28; Rev. 20:4).[38]  This contrast regarding thrones indicates that the 24 elders are distinct from redeemed human beings.

The fact that the 24 elders are seated on thrones in heaven and are distinct from redeemed human beings may indicate that they are the angels whom, as noted earlier, Paul called "thrones" in Colossians 1:16.[39]

Seventh, the 24 elders are consistently grouped with angels (Rev. 4:4, 6, 9-10; 5:6, 8, 11, 14; 7:11; 14:3; 19:4).[40]  In fact, Revelation 5:11 seems to indicate that they are a middle group of angels between the four living beings and the great angelic host. It appears that the four living beings are closest to the throne of God, the 24 elders are immediately beyond them, and the great host of angels is immediately beyond the elders.

Eighth, one of the 24 elders served as a messenger and an interpreter of divine revelation for the Apostle John (Rev. 5:5; 7:13-17).[41]  The Bible consistently indicates that these are the functions of angels to God's human spokesmen (Dan. 8:16-26; 9:21-27; Rev. 1:1; 17:1-3; 22:6-8).

Ninth, John called the elder who interpreted divine revelation "lord" (the word translated "Sir" in Rev. 7:14 is *kurios,* which means *lord*).[42] This term is used by a speaker when addressing a person of higher rank than himself.[43] The fact that John called one of the 24 elders "lord" indicates that he recognized that the messenger was of higher rank than he.

In light of the fact that John was an apostle of Jesus Christ and, therefore, of the highest rank of the church's leadership, this recognition has significant implications. Because the 24 elders were of higher rank than an apostle of Jesus Christ, the apostles could not be part of the elders. In addition, surely no redeemed human beings are of a higher rank than an apostle of Jesus Christ. With this understanding, and the fact that the elders were of higher rank than an apostle, it must be concluded that the 24 elders were of a higher rank than redeemed human beings. This makes them distinct from redeemed human beings.

It is obvious that John was not addressing deity when he called one of the 24 elders "lord." This indicates that the 24 elders belonged to an order of beings higher in rank than human beings but lower than God. In light of this, it is interesting to note that another man applied the same designation of "Lord" to an angel when he appeared to him (Acts 10:1-4).[44]

Tenth, the 24 elders are related to the prayers of saints in the same or a similar way as an angel (Rev. 5:8; 8:3-4; cp. Ps. 141:2).[45]

Eleventh, the 24 elders wear white garments (Rev. 4:4). Although it is true that the redeemed human beings in heaven wear white garments (Rev. 6:9-11; 7:9-14), the Bible clearly indicates that angels also wear white garments (Mt. 28:3; Mk. 16:5; Jn. 20:12; Acts 1:10).

Twelfth, the Book of the Revelation never indicates that the 24 elders represent a larger group.[46]

Thirteenth, the 24 elders are located around the throne of God, have a special relationship with Him as His favorites, praise and revere Him when the four living beings emphasize the uniqueness or holiness of God, and acknowledge that they cannot be compared to Him. It appears that they are a significant part of the great angelic council of heaven noted earlier in Psalm 89:5-7. The holy angels of that council surround the unique presence and throne of God in heaven. They also have a special relationship with God, for they are trusted intimates to whom God reveals His secret plans and purposes, and they praise and reverence Him, acknowledging that He is holy or unique and that they cannot be compared to Him.

## ENDNOTES

[1] R.D. Patterson, "sode," *Theological Wordbook of the Old Testament*, Vol. II, ed. by R. Laird Harris, Gleason L. Archer, Jr., and Bruce K. Waltke (Chicago: Moody Press, 1980), p. 619.

[2] Joseph Addison Alexander, *The Psalms* (Grand Rapids: Zondervan Publishing House, n.d.), p. 370.

[3] Franz Delitzsch, *Biblical Commentary on the Psalms*, Vol. III, trans. by Francis Bolton (Grand Rapids: Wm. B. Eerdmans Publishing Company, 1959), p.36.

[4] Alexander, *The Psalms*, p. 370.

[5] Willem A. VanGemeren, "Psalms," *The Expositor's Bible Commentary*, Vol. 5, ed. by Frank E. Gaebelein (Grand Rapids: Zondervan Publishing House, 1991), p. 576.

[6] Delitzsch, *Biblical Commentary on the Psalms*, Vol. I, p. 368; see also, Vol. III, p. 36.

[7] R.D. Patterson, "sabiyb," *Theological Wordbook of the Old Testament*, Vol. II, ed. by R. Laird Harris, Gleason L. Archer, Jr., and Bruce K. Waltke (Chicago: Moody Press, 1980), p. 615.

[8] Alexander, *The Psalms*, p. 371.

[9] *Ibid.*

[10] John E. Hartley, "sebaoth," *Theological Wordbook of the Old*

*Testament*, Vol. II, ed. by R. Laird Harris, Gleason L. Archer, Jr., and Bruce K. Waltke (Chicago: Moody Press, 1980), p. 750.

[11] William Owen Carver, "seraphim," *The International Standard Bible Encyclopaedia*, Vol. IV, ed. by James Orr (Grand Rapids: Wm. B. Eerdmans Publishing Company, 1957), p. 2732.

[12] For an in-depth treatment of this concept, see two articles on the holiness of God by Renald E. Showers in the December 1986/January 1987 and February/March 1987 issues of the magazine *Israel My Glory*, published by The Friends of Israel Gospel Ministry, Bellmawr, NJ.

[13] William F. Arndt and F. Wilbur Gingrich, *A Greek-English Lexicon of the New Testament* (Chicago: The University of Chicago Press, 1957), p. 752.

[14] R. Laird Harris, "sarap," *Theological Wordbook of the Old Testament*, Vol. II, ed. by R. Laird Harris, Gleason L. Archer, Jr., and Bruce K. Waltke (Chicago: Moody Press, 1980), p. 884.

[15] For example, William F. Arndt and Wilbur F. Gingrich, *A Greek-English Lexicon of the New Testament*, p. 148.

[16] Abraham Cohen, *Everyman's Talmud* (New York: Schocken Books, 1995), p. 50.

[17] William F. Arndt and F. Wilbur Gingrich, *A Greek-English Lexicon of the New Testament*, p. 7.

[18] Gerhard von Rad, "aggelos," *Theological Dictionary of the New Testament*, Vol I, ed. by Gerhard Kittel, trans. and ed. by Geoffrey W. Bromiley (Grand Rapids: Wm. B. Eerdmans Publishing Company, 1969), p. 77.

[19] Franz Delitzsch, *Biblical Commentary on the Book of Job*, Vol. I (Grand Rapids: Wm B. Eerdmans Publishing Company, 1956), p. 53.

[20] Charles D. Isbell, "ir," *Theological Wordbook of the Old*

*Testament,* Vol. II, p. 1055.

[21] Gleason L. Archer, Jr., "Daniel," *The Expositor's Bible Commentary*, Vol. 7, p. 61.

[22] For example, see William F. Arndt and F. Wilbur Gingrich, "thronos," "kuriotes," *A Greek-English Lexicon of the New Testament,* pp. 365, 461.

[23] F. F. Bruce, *Commentary on the Epistle to the Colossians* in *The New International Commentary on the New Testament*, ed. by F. F. Bruce (Grand Rapids: Wm. B. Eerdmans Publishing Company, 1975), p. 198.

[24] William F. Arndt and F. Wilbur Gingrich, *A Greek-English Lexicon of the New Testament*, p. 446.

[25] A. Skevington Wood, "Ephesians," *The Expositor's Bible Commentary*, Vol. 11, p. 86.

[26] E. K. Simpson, *Commentary on the Epistle to the Ephesians* in *The New International Commentary on the New Testament*, ed. by F. F. Bruce (Grand Rapids: Wm. B. Eerdmans Publishing Company, 1975), p. 143.

[27] *Ibid.,* footnote, p. 75.

[28] William F. Arndt and F. Wilbur Gingrich, *A Greek-English Lexicon of the New Testament*, p. 732.

[29] Otto Schmitz, "thronos," *Theological Dictionary of the New Testament,* Vol. III, ed. by Gerhard Kittel, trans. and ed. by Geoffrey W. Bromiley (Grand Rapids: Wm. B. Eerdmans Publishing Company, 1968), p. 167.

[30] Robert L. Thomas, *Revelation 1-7* (Chicago: Moody Press, 1992), p. 410.

[31] *Ibid.*

[32] Gunther Bornkamm, "presbuteros," *Theological Dictionary of*

*the New Testament*, Vol. VI, ed. by Gerhard Friedrich, trans. and ed. by Geoffrey W. Bromiley (Grand Rapids: Wm. B. Eerdmans Publishing Company, 1973), p. 668.

[33] Carl Schneider, "kathemai," *Theological Dictionary of the Old Testament*, Vol. III, ed. by Gerhard Kittel, trans. and ed. by Geoffrey W. Bromiley (Grand Rapids: Wm. B. Eerdmans Publishing Company, 1968), p. 441.

[34] *Ibid.*, p. 442.

[35] Otto Schmitz, "thronos," *Theological Dictionary of the New Testament*, Vol. III, p. 162.

[36] *Ibid.*, p. 166.

[37] *Ibid.*

[38] Robert L. Thomas, *Revelation 1-7*, p. 346.

[39] F. F. Bruce, *Commentary on the Epistle to the Colossians*, p. 198, footnote 84.

[40] Robert L. Thomas, *Revelation 1-7*, p. 348.

[41] Gunther Bornkamm, "presbuteros," *Theological Dictionary of the New Testament*, Vol. VI, p. 668.

[42] *Ibid.*

[43] Werner Foerster, "kurios," *Theological Dictionary of the New Testament*, Vol. III, ed. by Gerhard Kittel, trans. and ed. by Geoffrey W. Bromiley (Grand Rapids: Wm. B. Eerdmans Publishing Company, 1968), p. 1045.

[44] *Ibid.*, p. 1086.

[45] Robert L. Thomas, *Revelation 1-7*, p. 348.

[46] *Ibid.*, p. 347.

# 3

# THE RELATIONSHIPS OF ANGELS TO HUMAN BEINGS

The Bible relates several interesting facts regarding the relationships of angels to human beings.

**First, angels are greater in power than mortal human beings**. The Apostle Peter wrote about rebellious false teachers who purposely do risky things that even angels, who "are greater in power and might," do not do (2 Pet. 2:10-11). The Apostle Paul clearly taught that during this life Christians must rely on God's armor, not their own human power, to deal effectively with attacks by evil angels (Eph. 6:10-18). Through these presentations, both apostles were stating that angels are more powerful than mortal humans.

**Second, angels are higher on the scale of personal beings than mortal human beings.** There are three different kinds of personal beings existing in the universe: divine, angelic, and human. Because these three kinds differ from each other in nature and ability, we can legitimately say that together they form a *scale* of beings.

Both angelic and human beings worship the divine beings (God the Father, God the Son, and God the Holy Spirit) and thereby acknowledge that those beings are infinitely superior to themselves (Ps. 89:5-8; 148; Phil. 2:9-11; Rev. 4:8-11; 5:11-14). This indicates that the divine beings are at the top of the scale of personal beings.

King David addressed the following statements to God:

When I consider thy heavens, the work of thy fingers, the moon and the stars, which thou hast ordained, What is man, that thou art mindful of him? And the son of man, that thou visitest him? For thou hast made him a little lower than the angels (Ps. 8:3-5; cp. Heb. 2:6-7).

David clearly stated that angels in the supernatural realm are higher on the scale of personal beings than humans in the natural realm.

It can be concluded from these comments that the order on the scale of personal beings is as follows: At the top are the divine beings; at the bottom are human beings; in between the two are the angels.

**Third, holy angels are co-workers with human believers in the service of God.** On two different occasions, angels told the Apostle John that they were "fellow servants" together with him, New Testament prophets, and all true believers in Jesus (Rev. 19:10; 22:8-9). The fact that powerful holy angels and human believers serve the same divine Master means that believers are not alone in ministry. This truth should be a source of comfort and encouragement to all of God's saints on earth.

**Fourth, angels are never to be worshiped by human beings.**
Twice the Apostle John attempted to worship angels (Rev. 19:10;
22:8-9). The Greek construction of 19:10 indicates that John
intended to worship the angel as God.[1] Apparently in both
instances John was so overwhelmed by the supernatural nature of
these beings that he mistook them for divine beings.

Both angels immediately rejected worship of themselves and
strongly reprimanded John for trying to worship them. The
Greek construction of their immediate response, which is translated "See thou do it not," indicates that they felt very strongly
that angels should never be worshiped.[2]

With a sense of urgency, both angels commanded John to worship God.[3] They felt compelled to drive home the point that only
deity is to be worshiped. Their response signifies that angels are
not deity.

In order to make it very clear that they did not belong to the
realm of deity, both angels gave a reason why they were not to be
worshiped. They were only servants of God, the same as John,
the New Testament prophets, and all true believers in Jesus. This
declaration indicates that God is superior to the angels. He is
their sovereign Lord or Master. It also means that angels are not
the highest beings of the universe.

Why would John record these humiliating experiences in the
Book of the Revelation that he would send to the seven churches
of Asia, which knew him so well (Rev. 1:11)? Robert L. Thomas,
commenting on Revelation 19:10, provides the following answer
to that question:

> The tendency toward angel worship had for some time
> fascinated the churches in the province of Asia (cf. Col.
> 2:18) and continued to linger in the area after NT times.
> So the writer deals decisively with the practice both here
> and in 22:8, even though he puts himself in a bad light in
> doing so. He sought to help others resist the tendency.[4]

The Apostle Paul also made it clear to his readers that they should not worship angels. Paul's statement in Colossians 2:18 indicates that one of the churches in Asia, the church in the city of Colosse, was being plagued by false teachers who had established a cult involving the worship of angels.[5]

**Fifth, in the future believers will judge angels.** In 1 Corinthians 6:3 the Apostle Paul said, "Know ye not that we shall judge angels?" It is possible to understand the word "judge" in two ways, either in the sense of condemning to punishment or in the sense of ruling over. For the latter, note Matthew 19:28, where Jesus indicated that during His millennial reign on earth the apostles will sit on twelve thrones "judging" (ruling) the twelve tribes of Israel.[6]

The Bible makes it clear that in the future evil angels will be condemned to suffer terrible punishment because of their wrong deeds (2 Pet. 2:4; Jude 6; Rev. 20:1-3, 10). If Paul intended the first possible meaning of the word "judge" in his statement, then he was saying that believers will assist in the future condemnation of the evil angels to that terrible punishment. Perhaps we shall condemn the evil angels who wage war against us during our mortal life on this earth (Eph. 6:11-12).

If Paul intended the second possible meaning, then he was saying that in the future believers, as glorified human beings, will rule or preside over the holy angels.[7] Because the future glorified humanity of believers in Jesus Christ will be made like His glorified humanity (1 Jn. 3:2), and because the glorified humanity of Jesus Christ has been exalted to a position of authority over the angels (Eph. 1:20-21; Phil. 2:8-11; Col. 2:10), the glorified humanity of believers will also be exalted to a position of authority over the angels. This may mean that in their future glorified state, believers will be moved above the angels on the scale of personal beings.

## ENDNOTES

[1] Robert L. Thomas, *Revelation 8-22* (Chicago: Moody Press, 1995), p. 380.

[2] *Ibid.*, p. 375.

[3] *Ibid.*, p. 377.

[4] *Ibid.*, p. 375.

[5] F. F. Bruce, *Commentary on the Epistle to the Colossians* in *The New International Commentary on the New Testament*, ed. by F. F. Bruce (Grand Rapids: Wm. B. Eerdmans Publishing Company, 1975), p. 247.

[6] Charles Hodge, *The First Epistle to the Corinthians* (London: The Banner of Truth Trust, 1959), pp. 95-96.

[7] *Ibid.*

# THE RELATIONSHIPS OF ANGELS TO JESUS CHRIST

The Bible presents several significant relationships of angels to Jesus Christ. Most of these relationships, when taken together, emphasize the fact that Jesus Christ is exalted above and infinitely superior to the angels.

## Jesus Christ Existed Before the Angels

As noted earlier, the church in Colosse was plagued by false teachers of a cult involving angel worship. The Apostle Paul wrote his epistle to the Colossians to refute that heresy. As a result, he recorded some very significant truths concerning the relationship of angels to Jesus Christ. One of those truths is the fact that Jesus Christ existed before the angels. Paul presented that truth in two ways.

First, in Colossians 1:15 Paul declared that Jesus Christ, who provided forgiveness of sins for human beings (v. 14), is "the first-born of all creation." Through this statement, Paul did *not* mean that Christ Himself was created, the first part of creation. Several specifics definitely rule out that meaning.

The context of Paul's statement "in the sharpest manner distinguishes Christ from creation."[1] Verse 16, which explains the expression "the first-born of all creation," teaches that Christ created *all* things that have been created, including the invisible "thrones, or dominions, or principalities, or powers" (v. 16) in heaven (which, as noted earlier, refer to angels). How could He have created *all* created things if He Himself were a created being?

Also, there was a different word meaning "first-created."[2] Paul did not use that word here. In fact, that word is never used of Christ in the Bible.

Finally, one of the connotations of the word "first-born" that Paul used was "priority in time."[3] Thus, through the expression "the first-born of all creation," Paul was indicating that Jesus Christ existed before everything that was created, including the angels.

A second way that Paul communicated the same truth was by declaring that Christ "is before all things" (v. 17). In this passage, the word translated "before" refers to Christ's pre-existence.[4] Since "all things" refers back to "all things . . . created" in verse 16, it can be concluded that when Paul declared that Christ "is before all things," he was asserting that Christ existed before everything that was created, including the angels.

## Jesus Christ is the Sovereign Lord Over the Angels

The word "first-born" that Paul used in the expression "the first-born of all creation" in Colossians 1:15 had another connotation: "supremacy over," in addition to "priority in time."[5] Thus, Paul was saying that Christ holds a position of supremacy over all of creation. He is the sovereign Lord of everything that has been created, including the angels

Paul asserted this same truth again in Colossians 2:10 when he wrote that Christ "is the head of all principality and power."

One aspect of Christ's sovereignty over angels was clearly demonstrated during His first coming: His authority to cast demons out of people (Lk. 4:41; 7:21) and to give that same authority to His apostles (Lk. 9:1) and the seventy (Lk. 10:1, 17). This authority demonstrated that Jesus Christ is the true Messiah, the one who will remove all demonic or evil angelic presence and influence from the earth when He establishes His future millennial reign (Isa. 24:21-23; Rev. 20:1-3).

## Jesus Christ Created the Angels

In Colossians 1:16 the Apostle Paul declared why Christ is the sovereign Lord over all creation, including the angels: "For by him were all things created...all things were created by him."

In the first part of his declaration, Paul's literal statement, "For *in* him all things were created," signifies that all of creation took place within the sphere of the person of Christ. None of it took place apart from Him. Curtis Vaughan explains it this way: "He was its conditioning cause, its originating center, its spiritual locality. The act of creation rested, as it were, in him."[7]

In the second part of his declaration, Paul's literal statement, "all things were created *through* him," means that Christ was the mediating agent through whom God brought the entire universe into existence.[8]

Both parts of Paul's declaration, when taken together, indicate that Jesus Christ is the person who created everything that has been created. The Apostle John declared the same truth: "All things were made by him; and without him was not anything made that was made" (Jn. 1:3).

Paul's inclusion of invisible angels of the heavenly realm in the "all things" of verse 16 indicates that the angels were created by Christ. This is one of the reasons He is sovereign Lord over them.

## The Angels Were Created for Jesus Christ's Benefit

At the end of Colossians 1:16, the Apostle Paul gave another reason why Christ is sovereign Lord over all of creation. He asserted that all things, including the angels, were created "for" Christ. This means that Christ is the goal or ultimate purpose for which every part of the created universe was brought into being and exists. Handley C. G. Moule expressed this truth as follows:

> Their final cause is to serve His will, to contribute to His glory; He who is their Creator is also their Goal. Their whole being, willingly or unwillingly, moves that way—to Him; whether, as His blissful servants, they shall be as it were His throne; or, as His stricken enemies, "His footstool."[9]

F. F. Bruce summarized the significance of Colossians 1:16 by saying, "Here the point is that the highest angel-princes, like the rest of creation, are subject to Christ as the One in whom, through whom and for whom they were created."[10]

## The Angels Are Sustained by Jesus Christ

In Colossians 1:17, the Apostle Paul stated (concerning Christ), "by him all things consist." Once again the "all things" is a reference to the "all things created," including the angels, of verse 16. The verb translated "consist" means "continue, endure, exist."[11] The verb is in the perfect tense, so in this context it refers to the continuing result of Christ's work of creation. The point is that not only did Christ bring every created thing into existence, but He also continues to sustain the existence of every created thing, including the angels.

Concerning this statement about Christ, F. F. Bruce wrote the following:

> This adds something to what has been said before about His agency in creation. He maintains in being what He has brought into being. Similarly, in Heb. 1:2 f. the Son of God is not only the One through whom the worlds were made but also the One who maintains them in being by His almighty and enabling word...for Paul it is the living Christ, who died to redeem men, that is the sustainer of the universe and the unifying principle of its life.[12]

This is yet another reason for His sovereign authority over all creation, including the angels.

## The Angels Are Commanded to Worship Jesus Christ

Hebrews 1:6 records the following command of God to angels regarding His Son Jesus Christ: "And let all the angels of God worship him." This command signifies several noteworthy things concerning Jesus Christ. First, because, as noted earlier, the Bible teaches that angels are never to be worshiped, this command by God clearly indicates that Christ is not an angel.

Second, a study of the New Testament usage of the word translated "worship" in this command indicates that it referred to an act of reverence, respect, or submission that an individual directed toward a person superior to himself. In light of this, the fact that God commanded the angels to worship Christ signifies that Christ is superior to the angels.

Third, the word translated "worship" in this command is used in other passages of the New Testament for the worship of deity by angelic and human creatures. For example, Jesus used that word for human beings worshiping God the Father (Jn. 4:21-24); the Apostle John used it for angels worshiping God the Father on His throne (Rev. 7:11); and angels used it when they commanded the

Apostle John to worship God but not angels (Rev. 19:10; 22:9).

An important conclusion is prompted when the fact that the New Testament uses this word for the worship of deity is combined with these following other facts: Christ is superior to the angels; God, not angels, is to be worshiped; Christ the Son is to receive equal honor with God the Father (Jn. 5:23); and John witnessed every creature in the universe directing exactly the same worship toward God the Father on His throne and Jesus Christ the Lamb (Rev. 5:13). The conclusion is that God's command to the angels to worship His Son indirectly ascribes deity to Jesus Christ.

## Jesus Christ Was Made a Little Lower Than the Angels

Because God created man a little lower than the angels on the scale of personal beings (Heb. 2:6-7), when Christ became a human being through His incarnation (Jn. 1:14), He too "was made a little lower than the angels" in the realm of His humanity (Heb. 2:9). Just think of the incredible implications of this truth. The very person who existed before the angels, who created and sustains them, who is their sovereign Lord, for whose benefit they exist, and whom they are to worship allowed Himself to be made a little lower than they in the human aspect of His being, which He obtained through incarnation.

Why did Christ, the Creator, Sustainer, and sovereign Lord of the universe, allow Himself to be made a human, lower than His angelic creatures? So that He could die as a substitute for all human beings and thereby make reconciliation for their sins, free them from the power and enslaving fear of death, and help them when they are tempted (Heb. 2:9, 14-18).

Love motivated Christ to do this (Gal. 2:20; Eph. 5:2). He was so much more concerned for the welfare of His rebellious, sinful human creatures than for His own welfare that He voluntarily laid aside all the glories and privileges of heaven, which He had enjoyed with the Father as the Son of God from eternity past, entered the humbling experience of becoming a human being on earth through incarnation, and allowed His reputation to be ruined by dying on a cross, the form of death that the ancient world scornfully called "the slaves' death"[13] (Phil. 2:3-8; Jn. 10:15-18; 15:13).

All human beings have sinned and become subject to God's judgment (Rom. 3:10, 23), and there are no works that people can do to cancel out their sins and make themselves right with God (Isa. 64:6; Eph. 2:8-9; Ti. 3:5-6). Therefore, Christ knew that the only way for human beings to be saved from the penalty of their sins and made right with God was for Him to become a human being, die as a substitute to pay the penalty for the sins of the whole human race, be buried, and then be resurrected bodily from the dead (1 Cor. 15:1-4). Then human beings would have to place personal faith (trust) totally and exclusively in Him as their crucified, buried, and risen Savior (Jn. 3:16-18; Rom. 3:20-28; Gal. 2:16).

Love motivated Christ to allow Himself to be made a little lower than the angels so that He could provide the only way of eternal salvation available to human beings and acceptable to God (Jn. 14:6; Acts 4:12). What an incredible thing He did for our sake! He paid a debt He did not owe to free us from a debt we could not pay. This should cause us to fall before Him in gratitude and devotion.

## Jesus Christ Defeated and Openly Shamed Evil Angels in the Cross

After talking about the cross at the end of the preceding verse, Paul in Colossians 2:15 wrote, "And, having spoiled principalities and powers, he made a show of them openly, triumphing over them in it." To understand this statement, we must first examine its immediate context.

*Bethel Baptist Church*
P.O. BOX 167
AUMSVILLE, OR 97325

**Colossians 2:14**:  Having referred to God's gracious forgiveness of all the transgressions of believers in Christ (end of v. 13), Paul presented the basis of that forgiveness in verse 14.  God is able to forgive all sin because of something significant that Christ accomplished on the cross.  Through His death He blotted "out the handwriting of ordinances that was against us, which was contrary to us, and took it out of the way, nailing it to his cross."

The word translated "handwriting" refers specifically to "a certificate of indebtedness."[14]  Paul indicated that this document of indebtedness was related to "the ordinances" (literal translation), a reference to God's holy ordinances contained in the Mosaic Law.[15]  In Romans 3:19-20, Paul taught that instead of the Law being a means of justification, it is an instrument of condemnation.  It exposes the sins of all human beings (see Rom. 7:7), demonstrates their guilt before the sinless God, and effectively silences any excuses they may try to offer for their wrong deeds.

Thus, the document of indebtedness to which Paul referred was the written record of every violation of God's holy ordinances committed by all human beings.  It was "the writing which witnesses against man 'in virtue of the ordinances'. . . a writ of accusation based on the Law."[16]  That document was a continuing threat because, as a written record, it was always available to God as a reminder of the sins of His human creatures and, therefore, of the debt they owed Him.  For that reason Paul said that it "was against us" and "was contrary to us."  It is interesting to note that ancient Judaism also taught "that God keeps an account of man's debt."[17]

In two different ways Paul indicated that Jesus Christ eliminated this threat through His death on the cross.  First, Christ did it by "blotting out the handwriting."  The word translated "blotting out" means to "remove, destroy, obliterate."[18]  While on the cross, Christ eliminated this threat by removing, destroying, or obliterating the written record of our sins that was against us.

Second, Christ "took" the document of indebtedness "out of the way." The verb translated "took" embodies the idea of "to carry off."[19] Christ eliminated the threat by carrying off the document of indebtedness "out of the way."

At this point we must ask, Out of the way of what? The word translated "way" means "midst, middle, center."[20] This word is used three times in Revelation (4:6; 5:6; 7:17) in the expression "the midst of the throne" to refer to the area immediately before the throne of God in heaven. As noted earlier, the document of indebtedness was a continuing threat because, as a written record, it was always available to God as a reminder of the sins of His human creatures and of the debt they owed Him. It therefore appears that before Christ's death, that document was located immediately before God's throne in heaven. Paul was saying that there is a genuine sense in which Christ carried off the document of indebtedness from its location immediately before God's throne in heaven and thereby eliminated it as a threat.

It should be noted that Paul used the Greek perfect tense for the verb translated "took." He did this to emphasize that Christ's work of carrying off the document of indebtedness was completed in the past and has lasting results. His removal of the written record of our sins before God's throne is permanent. Never again can it threaten us with alienation from God.

At the end of verse 14, Paul related that Christ carried off the document of indebtedness by "nailing it to his cross." Through His death on the cross, He paid in full our debt of sin and thereby put to death the written record of our sins, the document that continually reminded God of the debt we owed Him

John the Baptist used similar language when he foretold what Christ would accomplish through His sacrificial death on the cross: "Behold the Lamb of God, who taketh away the sin of the world" (Jn. 1:29). It is interesting to note that the word translated "taketh away" in John's statement is the same word that Paul used for Christ's carrying off the written record of all human sins through His death on the cross.

We can conclude from this that verse 14 describes work that Christ accomplished through His death on the cross, the work that enabled God to forgive all sins.

**Colossians 2:15**: Having examined the immediate context of Colossians 2:15, what bearing does this knowledge have upon the meaning of the verse? Paul began verse 15 by declaring that Christ "spoiled principalities and powers." In an earlier chapter we noted that the terms "principalities" and "powers" refer to angels. Because it would not be necessary for Christ to spoil holy angels, we must conclude that Paul was saying that Christ spoiled evil angels. But in what sense did He spoil them?

The combination of two details answers that question. First, the language of verse 15 seems to imply a connection between Christ's spoiling of evil angels and His work of putting to death the document of indebtedness that was a threat to human beings.[21] Second, the word translated "spoiled" literally means "stripped" and in this context carries the idea of "disarmed."[22] In other words, "the imagery is that of a conquered antagonist being stripped of his weapons and armor."[23]

The combination of these two details prompts the conclusion that before Christ's death, evil angels used the document of indebtedness as a weapon against human beings. As agents of Satan, the accuser (Rev. 12:10), they tried to use this written record of human sins to stir up God's wrath to the point that He would stop saving humans out of Satan's kingdom (Col. 1:13) and perhaps even disown those whom He had already saved. It is interesting to note Paul's comments in Romans 8:38-39, which indicate that evil angels have made attempts to separate believers from God's love. Thus, evil angels used the document of indebtedness as a weapon to try to keep humans in Satan's kingdom.

Paul was saying that Christ spoiled these evil angels in that He disarmed or stripped them of this weapon when He destroyed or put to death the document of indebtedness through His death on the cross. Page expressed this truth as follows: "Christ's death on the cross deprived the powers of their ability to demand a guilty verdict and its accompanying penalty for humanity."[24]

Paul stated that once Christ had disarmed these evil angels of this weapon, He "made a show of them openly." In other words, Christ "exposed them to public disgrace."[25] According to Paul, Christ did this by "triumphing over them in it." The word translated "triumphing over" means to "lead in a triumphal procession someone as a captive."[26] It was the term used in the ancient world for the action "of a triumphant general leading a parade of victory. The conqueror, riding at the front in his chariot, leads his troops through the streets of the city. Behind them trails a wretched company of vanquished kings, officers, and soldiers— the spoils of battle."[27]

It appears that Paul was saying in verse 15 that after Christ (through His death) had disarmed evil angels of their weapon by destroying the document of human indebtedness, He exposed them to public disgrace by exhibiting them as defeated enemies in a victory parade before the whole spirit realm. In that parade, Christ was the triumphant conqueror. The cross was His chariot. The defeated captives who trailed behind in shame were the evil angels who had used the document as a weapon against human beings.

It may be that Christ led this *victory parade* while on the cross between the time of His death and the removal of His body. Outwardly, the cross appeared to be an instrument of great degradation and defeat for Christ, but in reality, because of what He accomplished on it through His death, it became His "chariot of victory".[28]

In relationship to the concept that Christ exhibited these evil angels as defeated enemies before the whole spirit realm, it is interesting to note that the Scriptures teach that angels watch what transpires on the earth (1 Cor. 4:9; Eph. 3:10; 1 Tim. 5:21). In addition, concerning Paul's statement in 1 Timothy 3:16 that Christ was "seen of angels," William F. Arndt and F. Wilbur Gingrich commented, "the triumphant Christ appears to the angelic powers."[29]

As other evil angels watched this defeat and humiliation of some of their powerful associates by Christ, they must have shuddered. This spectacle had twofold significance for them. First, it was an ominous portent of the defeat and humiliation by Christ that awaits them in the future. Second, because this defeat involved the destruction of a weapon that evil angels used to try to keep humans in Satan's kingdom, it was a blow to Satan himself. It demonstrated that their master was vulnerable to defeat by Christ.

Earlier it was noted that Christ has sovereign authority over all of creation, including the principalities and powers, because all things were created in Him, by Him, and for Him. He continuously sustains all of creation, and He existed before all of creation (Col. 1:15-17). As a result of His defeat of the principalities and powers on the cross, Jesus Christ established a further basis for His sovereign authority over them.[30]

## Jesus Christ Was Exalted Above the Angels

**Ephesians 1:20-22**:   In Ephesians 1:20-22, Paul used four expressions to emphasize the fact that when Jesus Christ ascended to heaven after His resurrection from the dead, God exalted Him to a position of authority over all creation, including the angels.

First, God "set him at his own right hand in the heavenly places."  The seat at the right hand of an important person was "the place of honor."[31]  The fact that God seated Jesus Christ at

His right hand on His heavenly throne (see Rev. 3:21), the seat of ultimate authority over the whole universe, indicates that God was thereby honoring Him by exalting Him to a position of authority over all of creation. Peter emphasized this in his Pentecost message. He declared that when God exalted Jesus by seating Him at His right hand on His throne, He thereby made Him "Lord" (Acts 2:30-36). He emphasized it again in 1 Peter 3:22 when he wrote, concerning Jesus, "Who is gone into heaven, and is on the right hand of God, angels and authorities and powers being made subject unto him."

Second, when God seated Jesus Christ at His right hand, He thereby placed Him "Far above all principality, and power, and might, and dominion, and every name that is named, not only in this age, but also in that which is to come." The word translated "far above" means "(high) above" and refers to "rank, power" in this passage.[32] God gave Jesus a rank or power high above all created beings, including the angels, for the present and the future.

Third, God "hath put all things under his feet." The verb translated "hath put" is the same as the one translated "being made subject" in 1 Peter 3:22, as noted above. In the Bible, feet are sometimes used "as a symbol of power" and "to express subordination."[33] Thus, in this third expression Paul was referring "not only to the supremacy of Christ but also to the subjection of all things to him."[34]

Fourth, God "gave him to be the head over all things." The verb translated "gave" means "appoint" in this passage.[35] The word for "head" denotes "superior rank."[36] Thus, when Christ ascended to heaven, God appointed Him to a superior rank over all of creation.

**A Potential Problem**: The fact that God exalted Jesus Christ to a position of authority over all creation, including the angels, when He ascended to heaven after His resurrection from the dead seems to pose a problem. In an earlier section, which addressed the fact that Christ is the sovereign Lord over the angels, we noted (on the basis of Colossians 1:16) that Christ is that sovereign Lord because He created the angels, and He is the goal or ultimate purpose for which the angels were brought into existence and exist.

In light of these reasons for His sovereign position over the angels, we are forced to conclude that Christ was Lord over the angels from the moment they were created. This means that He had this position of authority over them several millennia before His incarnation in human flesh and ascension to heaven. In light of this, how could Paul in Ephesians 1:20-22 teach that God exalted Jesus Christ to a position of authority over the angels when He ascended to heaven after His resurrection from the dead? Isn't this a contradiction?

No, it is not. Christ's position of authority before His incarnation in human flesh and ascension existed totally in the realm of His deity. Two things indicate this. First, He had that position because He created the angels. Only deity can create angels; humanity cannot create them. Second, He had that position several millennia before His incarnation in human flesh—He had it while He was exclusively deity, before He became human.

By contrast, the exalted position of authority that God gave Jesus Christ when He ascended to heaven after His resurrection existed in the realm of His glorified humanity. On the basis of Psalm 8:3-5, the writer of Hebrews taught that God created man a little lower on the scale of personal beings than the angels, and that at the present time man does not have all things in subjection under his feet (Heb. 2:6-8). The writer also taught that because God created man this way, when Christ became a human being through His incarnation (Jn. 1:14), He too "was made a little lower than the angels" in the realm of His humanity (Heb. 2:9). Christ took on humanity so that He could die as a substitute for all human beings and thereby provide the only way of eternal salvation available to mankind and acceptable to God (Heb. 2:9, 14-18; Jn. 14:6; Acts 4:12).

It should be noted that when Paul in Ephesians 1:20-22 taught that God gave Jesus Christ an exalted position of authority over all creation, including angels, when He ascended to heaven, he based one of his expressions on Psalm 8. When Paul declared that God has put all things under Jesus Christ's feet (v. 22), he was quoting from Psalm 8:6. Psalm 8 refers to all things being put under the feet of man. Because this is so, Paul's application of this reference to Jesus Christ indicates that in Ephesians 1:20-22, he had the following concept in mind: When Jesus Christ ascended to heaven after His humanity was glorified through resurrection, an exalted position of authority over all creation, including the angels, was given to Him in the realm of His glorified humanity. A. Skevington Wood explained Paul's concept as follows:

> Psalm 8:6 (LXX) is clearly in his mind (cf. Heb. 2:8). The Psalmist affirms man's dominion on earth. Here Paul claims that Christ, as God's new man, has universal dominion. Man largely forfeited his status through sin but through Christ as the ideal man he is restored to his proper dignity.[37]

The humanity of Jesus Christ was "a little lower than the angels" from the time of His incarnation to the time of His bodily resurrection. But that same humanity, now in glorified form, has been exalted to a position of authority high above the angels. Now the angels are subject to Him, not just in the realm of His deity but also in the realm of His glorified humanity.

**Philippians 2:6-9**: Paul taught this same exaltation of Jesus Christ in Philippians 2. In verses 6 through 8 Paul asserted that although Christ was deity—equal in nature with God—He voluntarily emptied Himself of the outward display of His deity or divine glory in order to submit to the humiliation of incarnation in human flesh and death on a cross. Because He became a man and died a death that the ancient world contemptuously called "the slaves' punishment,"[38] most people rejected His claim of deity or equality with God (Jn. 5:17-18; 10:30-33; Mt. 27:39-44).

After expounding on Christ's humiliation through His incarnation and death on the cross (vv. 6-8), Paul presented the result of that humiliation (v. 9): God exalted Jesus Christ through two means. First, God "highly exalted him." The word translated "highly exalted" means to "raise someone to the loftiest height."[39] God gave Him the highest position that anyone can have in the universe. This is parallel to "set him at his own right hand in the heavenly places, Far above all principality, and power, and might, and dominion" (Eph. 1:20-21). Jesus of Nazareth, the man who was so humiliated before all of creation through His rejection and crucifixion, was raised by God to the position of authority over that creation. Werner Foerster expressed the significance of this as follows: "Session at the right hand of God means joint rule. It thus implies divine dignity, as does the very fact of sitting in God's presence."[40]

Second, God gave Him "a name which is above every name." This is parallel to "Far above...every name that is named, not only in this age, but also in that which is to come" (Eph. 1:21).

Several things militate against that given name being Jesus. First, because the giving of this name was part of the result of Christ's incarnation and death, it must have been given to Him after His death. By contrast, God gave Him the name "Jesus" before His birth (Mt. 1:21).

Second, the name Paul had in mind is so awesome and authoritative that it will cause all created persons to bow before and acknowledge the exalted position of the one bearing it (vv. 10-11). Although Christ bore the name Jesus while in the world, many people did not bow before Him and acknowledge who He was. In fact, many rejected Him (Jn. 1:11).

Third, the word translated "above" indicates that Paul was referring to the name that is more exalted, more excellent, more glorious than any other name.[41]  In other words, it is a unique name—not a common name shared by other human beings. By contrast, the name Jesus (the Greek form of Joshua) is not a unique name. It has been shared by many other men in both ancient and modern times (Acts 13:6; Col. 4:11).[42]

Fourth, the fact that this name "is above every name" indicates that it is the supreme or highest name of the universe. Only one name fits that description—Jehovah or Yahweh, the personal name of God. Because God is the supreme being of the universe, His personal name must be the supreme name.

Several things in the Scriptures indicate that Jehovah or Yahweh is the supreme name of God and, therefore, the supreme name of the universe.

First, the full form of that name appears 5,321 times and its contracted form 25 times in the Hebrew Old Testament.[43]  By contrast, Elohim appears 2,570 times[44] and Adonai 423 times.

Second, Moses and the people of Israel stated the following concerning God: "the LORD [Yahweh] is his name" (Ex. 15:3). God Himself said, "I am the LORD [Yahweh]: that is my name" (Isa. 42:8); "they shall know that my name is The LORD [Yahweh]" (Jer. 16:21); and "the LORD [Yahweh] is his name" (Jer. 33:2; Amos 5:8; 9:6).

Third, Psalm 148:13 exhorts every part of the created universe to praise "the name of the LORD [Yahweh]" because "his name alone is excellent." The word translated "excellent" refers to what is "inaccessibly high."[45] This means that no other name can ever approach the level of God's personal name. His name is uniquely supreme. It alone is the "name which is above every name."

Fourth, God gave the following command: "profane not my holy name...I am the LORD [Yahweh]" (Lev. 22:2, 32). The word translated "holy" describes what "is intrinsically sacred...It connotes that which is distinct from the common or profane."[46] Thus, in this command God indicated that His name is unique. It is distinct from what is common; therefore, it should not be made into a common name.

Fifth, God indicated that He is "jealous for" His "holy name" (Ezek. 39:25). The word translated "jealous" refers to deep emotion, "consuming zeal focused on" what "is loved," "zeal for one's own property."[47] Thus, God has deep, consuming zeal for His unique, uncommon name, Yahweh.

Sixth, the significance of God's personal name is indicated by the following biblical statements concerning it: "thy name is from everlasting" (Isa. 63:16); "Thy name, O LORD [Yahweh], endureth forever" (Ps. 135:13); "let all flesh bless his holy name forever and ever" (Ps. 145:21); "All nations whom thou hast made . . . shall glorify thy name" (Ps. 86:9); "I will make thy name to be remembered in all generations" (Ps. 45:17); "According to thy name, O God, so is thy praise unto the ends of the earth" (Ps. 48:10); "let us exalt his name together" (Ps. 34:3); "blessed be thy glorious name, which is exalted above all blessing and praise" (Neh. 9:5); "make mention that his name is exalted" (Isa. 12:4); "let thy name be magnified forever" (2 Sam. 7:26); "thy great name" (Josh. 7:9); "Glory ye in his holy name" (1 Chr. 16:10); "Give unto the LORD [Yahweh] the glory due unto his name" (1 Chr. 16:29); and "blessed be the name of the LORD [Yahweh]" (Job 1:21).

Seventh, the Hebrew Scriptures refer to God's personal name by the simple designation "the name" and indicate that God required the death penalty for any person who blasphemed "the name" (Lev. 24:11, 16). Both this simple designation and the required death penalty reveal the unique, important significance of the name Yahweh.

Eighth, in Philippians 2:11 Paul related one aspect of God's purpose for raising Jesus Christ to the highest position in the universe and giving Him the supreme or highest name of the universe: so that in the future "every tongue should confess that Jesus Christ is Lord."

In order to understand the significance of this confession, it is important to note that during the course of Old Testament history, Jews came to regard God's personal name Yahweh (written JHVH) too sacred to pronounce. Thus, whenever they came to that name in the Hebrew text of their Scriptures, they pronounced a substitute title. "Instead of JHVH the Name was pronounced *Adonai* (my Lord)."[48] Because of this practice, when, during the 200s and 100s B.C., Jewish scholars produced the Septuagint (designated by LXX)—the Greek language version of the Hebrew Old Testament—they used *kurios* (Lord), the Greek counterpart of the Hebrew title *adonai*, as the substitute for Yahweh, the personal name of God.[49] As a result, by New Testament times the title *kurios* (Lord) was commonly used as the substitute for God's personal name Yahweh and was intended to prompt people to think of that name and what it signified.

In light of this common substitution of *kurios* (Lord) for God's personal name Yahweh, it can be concluded that when Paul related that one aspect of God's purpose for raising Jesus Christ to the highest position in the universe and giving Him the supreme or highest name of the universe was so that in the future every tongue should confess that Jesus Christ is Lord, he was thereby indicating that in the future every tongue should confess that Jesus Christ is Yahweh. This means, then, that the "name which is above every name," which God gave to Jesus after His humiliation on earth, is the name Yahweh.

The implication of God's giving Jesus His own personal name after His humiliation on earth is discerned by observing the sig-

nificance of names in general and the name Yahweh in particular.
The significance of both was stated by Abraham Cohen:

> To the Oriental, a name is not merely a label as with us.
> It was thought of as indicating the nature of a person or
> object by whom it was borne. For that reason special
> reverence attached to "the distinctive Name" of the
> Deity which He had revealed to the people of Israel,
> viz. the tetragrammaton, JHVH.[50]

Thus, God's personal name Yahweh signified His nature of
absolute deity.

God's giving of His own personal name to Jesus after His
humiliation on earth indicated that in spite of the fact that Jesus
was a man who had a common human name, died on a cross, and
experienced rejection of His claims of deity, He had the same
nature of absolute deity as God. Steven Barabas pointed out that
in Bible times, "when a person gave his own name to another, it
signified the joining of the two in very close unity."[51] In this
instance, it signified that God and Jesus were joined in absolute
unity of nature. Jesus claimed that unity of nature when He
declared, "I and my Father are one" (Jn. 10:30).

All the things we have seen concerning the two means that God
used to exalt Christ prompt the following conclusion: By raising
Jesus to the position that implies divine dignity, and by giving
Him His own personal name, God clearly indicated that Jesus of
Nazareth—the very man who was humiliated through incarnation
in human flesh, rejection, and crucifixion—has the same nature
as Himself and therefore is absolute deity.

Paul's statements in verses 10 and 11 reveal that God purposely exalted Jesus through means that emphasize His deity so that
"at the name of Jesus" every created personal being in heaven, on
earth, and under the earth should bow before Him in worship and
acknowledge that Jesus Christ is God (see Ps. 95:1; Isa. 45:23).
God has purposed that in the future all angels and humans,

regardless of where they are located—including the evil ones in places of judgment—will pay this homage to the one He has exalted.

Paul emphasized that this worship and acknowledgment of deity will be done "in the name of Jesus" (literal translation). It will be done in the name that Christ bore as a man in the days of His humiliation on earth, the name that so many have opposed, despised, and rejected. Thus, through this homage all angels and humans—even the enemies of Jesus—will acknowledge that the man who was despised and rejected has been exalted over them.

Through all of this, God elevates the humanity and human name of Jesus from humiliation to glorification.

**Hebrews 1:3-4**: The writer of Hebrews also related the exaltation of Jesus Christ over angels in Hebrews 1:3-4 when he wrote:

> Who, being the brightness of his glory, and the express image of his person, and upholding all things by the word of his power, when he had by himself purged our sins, sat down on the right hand of the Majesty on high, Being made so much better than the angels, as he hath by inheritance obtained a more excellent name than they.

## ENDNOTES

[1] Curtis Vaughan, "Colossians," *The Expositor's Bible Commentary*, Vol. 11, ed. by Frank E. Gaebelein (Grand Rapids: Zondervan Publishing House, 1978), p. 184.

[2] Norman L. Geisler, "Colossians," *The Bible Knowledge Commentary, New Testament Edition*, ed. by John F. Walvoord and Roy B. Zuck (Wheaton, IL: Victor Books, 1983), p. 673.

[3] Wilhelm Michaelis, "prototokos," *Theological Dictionary of the New Testament*, Vol. VI, ed. by Gerhard Friedrich, trans. and ed.

by Geoffrey W. Bromiley (Grand Rapids: Wm. B. Eerdmans Publishing Company, 1968), p. 878.

[4] Bo Reicke, "pro," *Theological Dictionary of the New Testament*, Vol. VI, ed. by Gerhard Friedrich, trans. and ed. by Geoffrey W. Bromiley (Grand Rapids: Wm. B. Eerdmans Publishing Company, 1968), p. 687.

[5] Wilhelm Michaelis, "prototokos," *Theological Dictionary of the New Testament*, Vol. VI, p. 879.

[6] F. F. Bruce, *Commentary on the Epistle to the Colossians* in *The New International Commentary on the New Testament*, ed. by F. F. Bruce (Grand Rapids: Wm. B. Eerdmans Publishing Company, 1975), p. 194.

[7] Curtis Vaughan, "Colossians," *The Expositor's Bible Commentary*, Vol. 11, p. 182.

[8] *Ibid.*

[9] Handley C. G. Moule, *Colossian And Philemon Studies* (London: Pickering & Inglis Ltd., n.d.), p. 78.

[10] F. F. Bruce, *Commentary on the Epistle to the Colossians*, pp. 198-99.

[11] William F. Arndt and F. Wilbur Gingrich, *A Greek-English Lexicon of the New Testament*, 4th rev. ed. (Chicago: The University of Chicago Press, 1957), p. 798.

[12] F. F. Bruce, *Commentary on the Epistle to the Colossians*, p. 200.

[13] Martin Hengel, *Crucifixion* (Philadelphia: Fortress Press, 1977), pp. 51-63.

[14] William F. Arndt and F. Wilbur Gingrich, *A Greek-English Lexicon of the New Testament*, p. 889.

[15] Johannes Schneider, "stauros," *Theological Dictionary of the*

*New Testament*, Vol. VII, ed. by Gerhard Friedrich, trans. and ed. by Geoffrey W. Bromiley (Grand Rapids: Wm. B. Eerdmans Publishing Company, 1971), p. 577.

[16] *Ibid.*

[17] Eduard Lohse, "cheirographon," *Theological Dictionary of the New Testament*, Vol. IX, ed. by Gerhard Friedrich, trans. and ed. by Geoffrey W. Bromiley (Grand Rapids: Wm. B. Eerdmans Publishing Company, 1974), p. 435.

[18] William F. Arndt and F. Wilbur Gingrich, *A Greek-English Lexicon of the New Testament*, p. 272.

[19] Joachim Jeremias, "airo," *Theological Dictionary of the New Testament*, Vol. I, ed. by Gerhard Kittel, trans. and ed. by Geoffrey W. Bromiley (Grand Rapids: Wm. B. Eerdmans Publishing Company, 1964), p. 185.

[20] William F. Arndt and F. Wilbur Gingrich, *A Greek-English Lexicon of the New Testament*, p. 508.

[21] Sydney H. T. Page, *Powers of Evil* (Grand Rapids: Baker Books, 1995), p. 253.

[22] William F. Arndt and F. Wilbur Gingrich, *A Greek-English Lexicon of the New Testament*, p. 82.

[23] Curtis Vaughan, "Colossians," *The Expositor's Bible Commentary*, Vol. 11, p. 202.

[24] Sydney H. T. Page, *Powers of Evil*, p. 253.

[25] Curtis Vaughan, "Colossians," *The Expositor's Bible Commentary*, Vol. 11, p. 202.

[26] William F. Arndt and F. Wilbur Gingrich, *A Greek-English Lexicon of the New Testament*, p. 364.

[27] Curtis Vaughan, "Colossians," *The Expositor's Bible Commentary*, Vol. 11, p. 202.

[28] *Ibid.*

[29] William F. Arndt and F. Wilbur Gingrich, *A Greek-English Lexicon of the New Testament*, p. 582.

[30] F. F. Bruce, *Commentary on the Epistle to the Colossians*, p. 233.

[31] William F. Arndt and F. Wilbur Gingrich, *A Greek-English Lexicon of the New Testament*, p. 174.

[32] *Ibid.*, p. 847.

[33] Konrad Weiss, "pous," *Theological Dictionary of the New Testament*, Vol. VI, ed. by Gerhard Friedrich, trans. and ed. by Geoffrey W. Bromiley (Grand Rapids: Wm. B. Eerdmans Publishing Company, 1968), pp. 628-29.

[34] A. Skevington Wood, "Ephesians," *The Expositor's Bible Commentary*, Vol. 11, ed. by Frank E. Gaebelein (Grand Rapids: Zondervan Publishing House, 1978), p. 31.

[35] William F. Arndt and F. Wilbur Gingrich, *A Greek-English Lexicon of the New Testament*, p. 192.

[36] *Ibid.*, p. 431.

[37] A. Skevington Wood, "Ephesians," *The Expositor's Bible Commentary*, Vol. 11, p. 31.

[38] Martin Hengel, *Crucifixion* (Philadelphia: Fortress Press, 1977), p. 51.

[39] William F. Arndt and F. Wilbur Gingrich, *A Greek-English Lexicon of the New Testament*, p. 849.

[40] Werner Foerster, "kurios," *Theological Dictionary of the New Testament*, Vol. III, ed. by Gerhard Kittel, trans. and ed. by Geoffrey W. Bromiley (Grand Rapids: Wm. B. Eerdmans Publishing Company, 1965), p. 1089.

[41] William F. Arndt and F. Wilbur Gingrich, *A Greek-English*

*Lexicon of the New Testament*, p. 847.

[42] A. T. Robertson, *Paul's Joy in Christ* (New York: Fleming H. Revell Company, 1917), pp. 138-39.

[43] J. Barton Payne, "Yahweh, Yah," *Theological Wordbook of the Old Testament*, Vol. I, ed. by R. Laird Harris, Gleason L. Archer, Jr., and Bruce K. Waltke (Chicago: Moody Press, 1980), p. 210.

[44] Jack B. Scott, "Elohim," *Theological Wordbook of the Old Testament*, Vol. I, ed. by R. Laird Harris, Gleason L. Archer, Jr., and Bruce K. Waltke (Chicago: Moody Press, 1980), p. 44.

[45] Gary G. Cohen, "sagab," *Theological Wordbook of the Old Testament*, Vol. II, ed. by R. Laird Harris, Gleason L. Archer, Jr., and Bruce K. Waltke (Chicago: Moody Press, 1980), p. 871.

[46] Thomas E. McComiskey, "qadosh," *Theological Wordbook of the Old Testament*, Vol. II, ed. by R. Laird Harris, Gleason L. Archer, Jr., and Bruce K. Waltke (Chicago: Moody Press, 1980), p. 788.

[47] Leonard J. Coppes, "qana," *Theological Wordbook of the Old Testament*, Vol. II, ed. by R. Laird Harris, Gleason L. Archer, Jr., and Bruce K. Waltke (Chicago: Moody Press, 1980), p. 802.

[48] Abraham Cohen, *Everyman's Talmud* (New York: Schocken Books, 1995), p. 25.

[49] Gottfried Quell, "kurios," *Theological Dictionary of the New Testament*, Vol. III, ed. by Gerhard Kittel, trans. and ed. by Geoffrey W. Bromiley (Grand Rapids: Wm. B. Eerdmans Publishing Company, 1965), p. 1058.

[50] Abraham Cohen, *Everyman's Talmud*, p. 24.

[51] Steven Barabas, "name," *The New International Dictionary Of The Bible*, ed. by Merrill C. Tenney and J. D. Douglas (Grand Rapids: Zondervan Publishing House, 1987), p. 690.

# 5

# THE FALL OF ANGELS

## The Original State of Angels

God created all of the angels as sinless beings. We know this through the combination of two concepts. First, as noted earlier, the angels were created within the scope of the six days of creation of Genesis 1. Second, at the end of those six days, God's evaluation of "every thing that he had made" was that "it was very good" (Gen. 1:31). That evaluation indicates that sin was nonexistent in every part of His creation, including the angels, up to that point.

It should be noted, however, that the angels were not confirmed or locked into this original sinless state. We have seen that God created the angels as personal beings with intellect, emotions, and a will. They had the ability to make decisions of their own volition. Thus, the only way that they could become confirmed in sinlessness was if they, of their own volition, chose to remain loyal to God. It they chose to rebel against God, they would lose their sinlessness and be confirmed or locked into a sinful state.

## The Original State of an Exalted Angel

Isaiah 14 and Ezekiel 28 refer to proud human rulers of ancient Babylon and Tyre. However, some of the descriptive language in these passages cannot be applied to human beings. Let us examine examples of such language.

**Ezekiel 28:** In the midst of this passage concerning a proud human ruler of ancient Tyre, verse 12 states, "Thou sealest up the sum, full of wisdom, and perfect in beauty." The Hebrew words translated "Thou sealest up the sum" convey the meaning of "perfect example."[1] This verse describes a being who was the perfect example or model of a creature full of wisdom and beauty. In other words, he was the most magnificent of God's creatures. Because, as noted in an earlier chapter, mortal human beings are lower on the scale of personal beings than angels, no mortal human—including rulers of ancient Tyre—could be God's most magnificent creature.

Verse 13 indicates that this being had "been in Eden, the garden of God." Because the Garden of Eden was sealed long before Tyre was founded, no human ruler of that city-state was ever in Eden.

Verse 13 mentions "the day" on which this being was "created." The human rulers of Tyre were procreated through human parents, not created. Only two human beings—Adam and Eve—were created.

Verse 14 identifies this being as "the anointed cherub that covereth." We saw in an earlier chapter that cherubim are angels, probably of the highest rank, who have the function of covering the unique presence of God, as illustrated by the ark of the covenant. The designation "the anointed cherub" seems to indicate that this being was the most exalted of the highest rank of angels. Because, as noted in an earlier chapter, mortal humans are lower than angels on the scale of personal beings, how could this be the identification of a human ruler of ancient Tyre?

Verse 15 makes the following assertion concerning this being: "Thou wast perfect in thy ways from the day that thou wast created, till iniquity was found in thee." The word translated "perfect" carries the meaning of "upright."[2] The word for "iniquity" refers "to behavior contrary to God's character."[3] In light of these meanings, verse 15 asserts that there was a period of time after this being's creation when he was not guilty of behavior contrary to God's character. In other words, for the first part of his existence this being was sinless, but there was a later point when he defiled himself with behavior contrary to God's character. Because all descendants of Adam, conceived and born through natural means, are in a state of sin from the time of their conception (Ps. 51:5), there is no time period in their mortal existence on earth when they are sinless. Thus, verse 15 cannot be an assertion concerning any of the pagan rulers of ancient Tyre.

Verse 14 indicates that while this being was sinless, he was "upon the holy mountain of God" and "walked up and down in the midst of the stones of fire." Some Old Testament scholars assert that in this specific passage, the expression "the holy mountain of God" refers to God's dwelling place in heaven.[4] Thus, this being lived in heaven with God while in his sinless state.

This understanding is supported further by the assertion that he "walked up and down in the midst of the stones of fire." In Bible times, God used fire to reveal His presence.[5] Fire was associated with His presence in heaven. Daniel was given a vision of God seated upon His throne in heaven (Dan. 7:9-10). That chariot-throne and its wheels had the appearance of fire, and a stream of fire flowed out from before Him in the midst of a great host of angels who stood before Him. Apparently those angels stood on the stream of fire in God's presence.

It should be noted that cherubim were closely related to the fire associated with God's presence. In a vision of His glorious presence that God gave to Ezekiel (Ezek. 1), the prophet saw four living creatures (identified as cherubim in Ezek. 10) come out of the midst of fire (vv. 1, 4-5). These cherubim had the appearance of coals of fire; fire moved up and down among them (v. 13); and coals of fire were centrally located under them (10:2, 6-7). The four cherubim formed a fast moving, living chariot for God and His throne (1:15-28). God had the visionary likeness of a man, fiery in appearance and surrounded by fire (vv. 26-27).

We have seen that fire was associated with God's presence in heaven and that cherubim were closely related to the fire associated with God's presence. The being of Ezekiel 28:14, while in his original sinless state, walked up and down in the midst of the stones of fire and is called a cherub. This seems to indicate that in the early part of his existence he lived in the presence of God in heaven. No human ruler of ancient Tyre lived in the presence of God in heaven.

**Isaiah 14:** In the midst of this passage concerning a proud human ruler of ancient Babylon, verse 12 declares, "How art thou fallen from heaven." The language of this declaration implies that the subject of this verse is a being who originally lived in heaven but then experienced a fall from there. No human ruler of ancient Babylon originally lived in heaven.

Verse 12 refers to this being as, "O Lucifer, son of the morning." The name Lucifer does not appear in the Hebrew text. It is a Latin translation of the Hebrew word *helel*, which is in the text. The Hebrew word means "shining one."[6] The root of this word "represents the giving off of light by celestial bodies."[7]

The designation "son of the morning" is the Hebrew way of calling this being the "morning star."[8] The word translated "morning" means "dawn" and refers to "the breaking of the day, that time just prior to sunrise."[9] The morning star is so much brighter than all other stars that when the light of dawn makes all other stars invisible, the morning star is still visible.

The point of these designations is that the subject of verse 12 is a shining being of light. Just as the morning star is the brightest of all stars, so this being is the brightest of all shining beings of light created by God.

This point is significant due to several facts. As noted earlier, God called angels "stars" (Job 38:7). The Bible portrays angels, not mortal humans, as bright shining beings (Mt. 28:2-3; Rev. 10:1). The Apostle Paul called Satan "an angel of light" (2 Cor. 11:14).

In light of what has been seen, it can be concluded that Isaiah 14:12 is not referring to a human ruler of ancient Babylon. Instead, its subject is the brightest or greatest of all the angels who originally had heaven as his home.

**Conclusion:** Much of the content of Ezekiel 28 and Isaiah 14 refers to proud human rulers of ancient Tyre and Babylon, but we have examined some descriptive language from both passages that cannot be applied to human beings. That language describes the brightest, most magnificent being created by God. God made him the highest of the angelic rank of cherubim, sinless in nature, and the perfect model of a creature of wisdom and beauty. He was given the privilege of covering the presence of God in heaven. Such was the original state of this exalted angel. Tragically, he did not keep that state.

## The Fall of This Exalted Angel

As noted earlier, according to Ezekiel 28:15 this exalted angel was sinless for the first part of his existence, but at a later point he defiled himself with behavior contrary to God's character. Two biblical passages shed light on the cause of this radical change.

First, Ezekiel 28:17 states, "Thine heart was lifted up because of thy beauty." In the Scriptures, the word *heart* usually refers to the inner control center of a personal being. It is the seat of the emotions (1 Sam. 2:1), the mind (Prov. 23:7), and the will (Dan. 1:8). Thus, all decisions are made in the heart.

When the Bible mentions the lifting up of the heart in an evil sense, as it does in Ezekiel 28, it is referring to inflating the inner control center with a disposition of pride (2 Chr. 26:16; 32:25-26). Because he was the most magnificent of God's creatures, this exalted angel willfully permitted his heart to be inflated with pride. Through this means, sin began in him, and he passed from a sinless state to a sinful state. Thus, pride was the cause of the radical change in this exalted angel.

In the second passage, in line with Ezekiel 28:17, the Apostle Paul indicated that the devil was "lifted up with pride" (1 Tim. 3:6).

By permitting his inner control center to be inflated with pride, this exalted angel corrupted his wisdom (Ezek. 28:17). In the Bible, wisdom in the ultimate sense is the same as ultimate reality. Ultimate reality consists of the following truths: There is only one God who actually exists. That God is the personal Creator and ultimate sovereign of the universe and everything in it. At the time of creation, He established a fixed order of natural and moral law and subjected the entire universe to that order (Prov. 1-9). Truly wise people bring themselves into harmony with ultimate reality by learning these truths, genuinely accepting them as valid, and allowing them to determine their philosophy of life, values, and conduct.

In his original sinless state, this exalted angel was the perfect model of a creature of wisdom. He was truly wise because he knew the truths of ultimate reality, accepted them as valid, and allowed them to determine his philosophy of life, values, and conduct. He thereby was in complete harmony with ultimate reality. But when he permitted his heart to be filled with pride, he stopped being a truly wise person, and his relationship to ultimate reality was radically changed.

Paul's statement about the devil being "lifted up with pride" helps to define this change (1 Tim. 3:6). The root of the word translated "pride" means "smoke."[10] Just as smoke blinds people to their surroundings, so pride blinds people to reality. Pride makes people believe that they are greater than they really are.

When this exalted angel became proud of his magnificent being, his pride blinded him to ultimate reality. Through pride he began to believe that he could be like God, as evidenced by his assertion, "I will be like the Most High" (Isa. 14:14). His pride blinded him to the ultimate reality that there is only one God who actually exists and is the ultimate sovereign of the universe and everything in it. No creature can become like God.

As a result of this radical change, God cast this exalted angel out of His heaven (Isa. 14:12; Ezek. 28:16) [the third heaven mentioned by Paul in 2 Cor. 12:2-4] down to the first heaven above the earth, where he now functions as "the prince of the power of the air" (Eph. 2:2). It appears that Jesus had this result in mind when He said, "I beheld Satan as lightning fall from heaven" (Lk. 10:18). Henry Alford declared that Jesus was referring "to the original fall of Satan, when he lost his place as an angel of light, not keeping his first estate."[11] The Apostle Paul also referred to the fall of the devil into judgment because of pride (1 Tim. 3:6).

Another result of this radical change is God renaming this exalted angel "Satan," which means "Adversary."[12] This was a very appropriate change of name because he had now become the ultimate enemy of God.

## The Time of Satan's Fall

When did Satan fall away from God? We noted earlier that sin was nonexistent in every part of God's creation, including the angels, through the end of the sixth or final day of creation (Gen. 1:31). Satan's fall therefore took place sometime after the end of creation. However, Satan was evil by the time he came to earth to tempt man to fall away from God (Gen. 3). These things prompt the conclusion that Satan's fall took place in the interval of time between the end of creation and the fall of man.

How long was that interval? It must have been quite short because when God created the first man and woman, He commanded them to be fruitful and multiply through procreation (Gen. 1:27-28), but there was no human conception until after the fall of man (Gen. 4:1).

## An Explanation

We have noted that much of the content of Ezekiel 28 and Isaiah 14 refers to proud human rulers of ancient Tyre and Babylon but that some of the language of both passages describes an exalted angel. Why do these Scriptures mix together descriptions of proud human rulers with those of a once exalted but now proud evil angel?

The Scriptures do this because Satan has a significant relationship with certain major human rulers during the course of world history. In an earlier chapter we saw that Ephesians 6:12 designates a specific class of evil angels as "the rulers of the darkness of this world." The term that is so translated means "world-ruler."[13] It refers to a being "who aspires to world control."[14] It identifies "unseen spiritual potentates who make human despots and false systems of thought their tools of dominion."[15] In other words, it refers to invisible, powerful, evil angels who influence and control powerful human rulers and movements for evil on earth.

Satan is the ultimate evil world ruler. In fact, he is the head of all evil angelic world rulers. To understand the implications of this, we must look at some significant events that transpired near the beginning of history. When God created man, He gave him dominion over all the earth and everything in it (Gen. 1:26).

Through this act, God established a theocracy as the original form of government for planet Earth. The term *theocracy* literally means *rule of God* and refers to the form of government in which the rule of God is administered by a representative. God ordained the first man, Adam, to be His representative, administering God's rule on His behalf over this earthly province of God's universal kingdom. Thus, God ruled the entire earth through one man.

We noted earlier that through pride Satan began to believe that he could be like God, and so he asserted, "I will be like the Most High" (Isa. 14:14). Because God was ruling the entire earth through one man, he too must rule the entire earth through one man. This became, and has continued to be, one of Satan's major goals throughout most of planet Earth's history.

Satan knew that to accomplish this goal, he somehow had to usurp the rule of the world system away from God. Genesis 3 records his means of doing that. Satan came to the earth in the subtle form of a serpent (Gen. 3:1; Rev. 20:2). He told the first two humans that if they would reject God and His rule, they would be like God (Gen. 3:5). This was the same thought that he adopted when he first sinned against God. He thereby succeeded in persuading Adam to fall away from God.

Through the fall of Adam, God lost His representative through whom He had been ruling the earth. As a result, the theocracy was lost, and Satan usurped the rule of the world system away from God. Several things indicate this radical change. Satan caused all the kingdoms of the world system to pass before Jesus, had the authority to give the rule of that system to any human he desired, and declared that the rule of the world system had been delivered to him (Lk. 4:5-6). The verb translated "delivered" is in the perfect tense. This is significant because it means that the rule of the world system was delivered to Satan in the past (by Adam), and that he and his forces continue to control the world system through the course of history. Because this is so, Jesus called Satan "the ruler of this world" (literal translation, Jn. 14:30); Paul called him "the god of this age" (2 Cor. 4:4); James warned that whoever is the friend of the present world system is "the enemy of God" (Jas. 4:4); and John stated that the whole world lies "in wickedness" (this could also be translated "in the evil one," 1 Jn. 5:19).

Usurping the rule of the world system away from God through the fall of man was the first step toward fulfilling Satan's goal of ruling the entire earth through one man. Throughout the course of history since the fall of man, Satan has progressively tried to move the world closer to a worldwide, one-man rule. Through the use of supernatural influence, either by himself (Isa. 14; Ezek. 28) or through his evil, angelic world rulers (Dan. 10:13, 20), he motivates human rulers—such as rulers of Tyre and Babylon—to try to build increasingly larger kingdoms or empires and thereby bring progressively larger areas of the world under one-man rule. Satan's final and greatest work along this line will be with the future Antichrist (2 Th. 2:3-10; Rev. 13:1-8).

On the basis of Isaiah 14, Ezekiel 28, 2 Thessalonians 2, and Revelation 13, it appears that Satan motivates these rulers toward worldwide, one-man rule by inflating their hearts with pride to the point that they believe they can be like God. Because God originally ruled the entire world through one man, they try to extend their rule over the whole earth. Thus, it is because Satan motivates these rulers with the same pride and belief factors that were true of him when he fell away from God that Isaiah 14 and Ezekiel 28 mix together descriptions of proud human rulers of ancient Babylon and Tyre with those of a once exalted but now proud evil angel.

In line with this understanding, Geoffrey W. Grogan wrote the following concerning this mixing together of descriptions of the ruler of Babylon with those of Satan in Isaiah 14:

> Nothing could be more appropriate, for the pride of
> the king of Babylon was truly satanic. When Satan

works his malign will through rulers of this world,
he reproduces his own wicked qualities in them, so
that they become virtual shadows of which he is
the substance.... All rulers of international significance whose overweening pride and arrogance
bring them to ruin under the hand of God's judgment illustrate both the satanic and the Antichrist
principles, for these principles are really one.[16]

## The Fall of Other Angels

In eternity past, God determined to establish a kingdom over
which He could rule as a sovereign king. This kingdom was to
be known as the Kingdom of God. In order to have a kingdom,
God had to have personal subjects who would serve Him. God
determined to create two kinds of personal subjects: angels to
serve Him primarily in the heavenly realm of His universal kingdom, and humans to serve Him in the earthly realm. As noted in
an earlier chapter, God created an enormous host of angels, all in
a holy or sinless state.

Because Satan wanted to be like God, and because God had a
universal kingdom over which He ruled as the sovereign king,
Satan determined that he too had to have a universal kingdom
over which he could rule as the sovereign king. Because God had
angels serving Him in His kingdom, Satan determined that he too
must have angels serving him in his kingdom. He, however, had
a problem. Because he was only a creature and not the Creator,
he lacked the ability to create other angels. The most he could
hope for was to persuade God's angels to join him in rebellion
against God.

Satan succeeded in persuading a significant number of the
angels to join him. We know this because the Scriptures refer to
Satan "and his angels" (Mt. 25:41; Rev. 12:7-9) and indicate that
he is the ruler over evil angels (Mt. 12:24-26).

The Bible does not give the exact number of angels who fell away from God, but it appears that Revelation 12:4 gives the proportion of those who followed Satan. That passage states that Satan "drew the third part of the stars of heaven and did cast them to the earth." We noted earlier that God called angels "stars" in Job 38:7. Robert L. Thomas wrote concerning the Revelation 12:4 statement:

> The stars must refer to angels who fell with Satan in history past. The similarity of this verse to Dan. 8:10, where "the host of heaven" is an apparent reference to angels, shows this. Already in Revelation a star has pictured an angel (9:1). That factor along with the reference to Satan's angels in 12:8-9 adds credence to this explanation. This is a war in heaven that resulted in the casting of Satan and his angels to earth.... The casting of the stars to earth is his leading of these angels to a battle in which they were worsted, when he too was hurled down from his heavenly abode to earth.[17]

It is concluded, then, that one-third of the angels followed Satan and fell away from God. Because they personally made this choice to rebel, they thereby lost their sinless state and became permanently locked into a fallen, evil state.

The implications of Revelation 12:4 as noted, together with the implications of Genesis 1:31 noted earlier, prompt the conclusion that this fall of angels took place during the time interval between the end of the sixth day of creation and the fall of man.

Satan became the ruler of this host of fallen angels. Just as God had angelic subjects in His kingdom, Satan now had angelic subjects in his. In conjunction with this, it is interesting to note that when Satan rebelled against God and asserted, "I will be like the Most High" (Isa. 14:14), he also boasted "I will exalt my throne above the stars of God" (Isa. 14:13).

## Two Major Classifications of Angels

It is apparent that when Satan tried to persuade all of God's angels to join his rebellion, two-thirds of them decided to remain loyal to God. The Bible calls them the "holy" or "elect" angels (Dan. 4:13, 17; Mk. 8:38; 1 Tim. 5:21). Through their personal choice to remain faithful to God, they were confirmed or permanently locked into their sinless state.

The fall of one-third of the angels caused the great host of angels whom God had created to be divided into two major classifications: the holy angels in God's kingdom and the fallen, evil angels in Satan's kingdom.

## Two Subdivisions of the Fallen, Evil Angels

Through time, the major classification of fallen, evil angels developed into two subdivisions.

### The Fallen, Free Angels

The fallen, free angels dwell with Satan in the first heaven above the earth and are under his rule (Eph. 2:2; 6:12; Rev. 12:7-9). They are free to move about, even on the earth, to do Satan's evil work. The Bible calls them "demons" (Mt. 12:22-26).[18]

### The Fallen, Confined Angels

This second subdivision consists of evil angels who were fallen, free angels under Satan's rule for a period of time after the angelic fall. However, sometime later they committed another sin so grievous that God took away their freedom and removed them from Satan's rule by confining them in a terrible prison. Two New Testament passages specifically refer to this group.

**Second Peter 2:4**: In this passage the Apostle Peter wrote, "For if God spared not the angels that sinned, but cast them down to hell, and delivered them into chains of darkness, to be reserved unto judgment." Several things should be noted concerning these comments.

First, Peter was talking about a particular group of angels whom God had already confined and chained in a terrible place of darkness in the past before Peter wrote his epistles.

Second, Peter named this place of imprisonment. Our English translations call it "hell," but it should be noted that Peter did not use the New Testament word for hell (the word *Hades*). Instead, he used the word *Tartarus*. The ancient world understood Hades and Tartarus to be distinct from each other. Both the Greeks and Jewish apocalyptic writers thought of Tartarus "as a subterranean place lower than Hades where divine punishment was meted out."[19] In the Jewish *Book of Enoch* (xx.2), Tartarus is presented as the place of punishment for fallen angels.[20] Peter was indicating that these evil spirits are imprisoned in the deepest pit of gloom.

Second Peter 2:4 is the only place in the New Testament where this place of judgment is mentioned by its proper name, Tartarus; however, several other passages refer to it by its descriptive term, "the bottomless pit" (lit., *the abyss*). The word *abyss* means *unfathomably deep*, and Jewish apocalyptic writers described it as "the place in which runagate spirits are confined (Book of Jubilees 5:6 ff.; Book of Enoch 10:4 ff., 11 ff.; 18:11 ff. etc.; Jude 6; 2 Pet. 2:4)."[21]

When Jesus confronted the demon-possessed Gadarene man, the demons begged Him not to cast them into the abyss (literal translation) [Lk. 8:31]. The fact that these angels made this plea indicates that the fallen, free angels knew that the abyss existed, that God had already placed some of their fellow fallen angels there in judgment, and that it is a terrible place for evil angels to be cast. The angels who had possessed the Gadarene man were terrorized by the prospect that Christ might imprison them in the abyss.

Third, Tartarus is only the temporary place of judgment for the evil angels confined there. Peter indicated that they are kept there until the time of their final judgment. At the end of this earth's history, they, together with Satan and all fallen angels, will be placed in another place of judgment—the eternal lake of fire (Mt. 25:41; Rev. 20:10).

Fourth, Peter made it clear that these angels were already confined in Tartarus because of some sin they committed before he wrote his epistle. We are forced to conclude that this sin was not the original angelic rebellion against God because if it had been that sin, all of the fallen angels, including Satan, would have been confined in this place of judgment. It had to be a sin that only this particular group of fallen angels committed sometime after they and all the other fallen angels had rebelled against God. In addition, it had to be far more grievous than the sin of original angelic rebellion against God because it prompted more severe judgment than did the original angelic rebellion. In conjunction with this, Merrill F. Unger wrote,

> The fallen angels that are bound, on the other hand, are those described by Peter and Jude, as ostensibly guilty of such enormous wickedness as no longer allowed them to roam the heavenlies with their leader Satan and the other evil angels, but plunged them down to the strictest and severest confinement in Tartarus.[22]

What was the nature of this sin? The second New Testament passage concerning this group of confined angels sheds more specific light on this issue.

**Jude 6-7**: In this passage Jude indicated that the sin of this group of confined angels consisted of four actions.

First, they "kept not their first estate" (v. 6). The word translated "first estate" means "domain, sphere of influence."[23] These angels did not remain in the domain or sphere of influence that God intended for angels. They left it to become part of a domain or sphere of influence that God had not ordained for angels.

Second, they "left their own habitation" (v.6). The word translated "habitation" means "dwelling place" or "abode" and refers espe-

cially to the residence of angels in the heavens.[24]   These angels
deserted their dwelling place in the first heaven to live in another
location.

Third, they gave "themselves over to fornication" (v. 7).  The
beginning part of verse 7 says, "Even as Sodom and Gomorrah,
and the cities about them in like manner [the Greek text says, "in
like manner to these"], giving themselves over to fornication."
Some interpreters assert that verse 7 has no relationship to the
angels of verse 6.[25]   They insist that the words "to these" (in the
Greek text) of verse 7 refer back to the cities of Sodom and
Gomorrah, not to the angels of verse 6, and that Jude was saying
therefore that the cities about Sodom and Gomorrah gave themselves over to fornication in like manner to Sodom and
Gomorrah.  It must be noted, however, that the Greek word for
cities is feminine in gender.  By contrast, the gender of both the
Greek word translated "to these" in verse 7 and the word for
angels in verse 6 is masculine.  This means that "to these" in
verse 7 refers back to the angels of verse 6, not to the cities of
Sodom and Gomorrah.[26]   Thus, in verse 7 Jude was saying that
Sodom and Gomorrah and the cities about them sinned in like
manner as the angels of verse 6.

One of the ways in which they sinned in like manner was in
giving "themselves over to fornication."  This does not mean that
the angels engaged in homosexual relationships as the men of
Sodom, Gomorrah, and neighboring cities did.  The term *fornication* sometimes refers to any kind of sexual relationship forbidden by God (Eph. 5:3; Col. 3:5).[27]   Jude's point was that the men
of Sodom, Gomorrah, and neighboring cities entered into sexual
relationships forbidden by God (men with men) in the same manner as the angels of verse 6 entered into sexual relationships forbidden by God (angels with human women).

Fourth, they went "after strange flesh" (v. 7).  They went after
flesh that God intended to be foreign to them.  To "go after

strange flesh = indulge in unnatural lust."[28]

The men of Sodom and Gomorrah and neighboring cities went after flesh that God intended to be foreign to them. Their homosexual relationships were unnatural. God created human males to have sexual relationships with human females (Gen. 2:18, 21-24; Mt. 19:4-6). He thereby indicated His intention that human males be sexually foreign to other human males (Lev. 18:22; 20:13; Dt. 23:17).

In like manner, the angels of verse 6 went after flesh that God intended to be foreign to them. As noted in an earlier chapter, God created angels as spirit beings without a physical body of flesh and bones. As a result, sexual relationships with physical flesh are contrary to the nature of angels. This indicates that God intended physical flesh to be sexually foreign to angels. The angels of verse 6, contrary to their nature and what God intended, pursued sexual relationships with physical flesh.

At the end of verse 6 Jude indicated the consequence of this fourfold sin by these angels. God put them in bonds in a gloomy place of darkness, where He keeps them until their final judgment at the end of this earth's history.

**Conclusion**:   A comparison of 2 Peter 2:4 with Jude 6-7 prompts the conclusion that both Peter and Jude were writing about the same group of angels and their sin. Most biblical scholars agree with this conclusion

Earlier we gave reason for concluding that the sin and confinement of this group of angels took place sometime after the original angelic rebellion against God. The fact that Peter and Jude referred to this sin and confinement in the past indicates that these things happened before they wrote their epistles. The interval between the original angelic rebellion and the writing of these New Testament epistles is considerable. Is it possible to identify more specifically the time and other particulars related to this angelic sin and confinement? To find the answer to this question, we must examine another issue.

# The Issue of Genesis 6

In Genesis 6:1-2, 4 Moses wrote,

> And it came to pass, when men began to multiply
> on the face of the earth, and daughters were born
> unto them, That the sons of God saw the daughters
> of men that they were fair; and they took them
> wives of all whom they chose...the sons of God
> came in unto the daughters of men, and they bore
> children to them, the same became mighty men
> who were of old, men of renown.

In this passage, Moses referred to activities that transpired on the earth before the Noahic flood.

Bible scholars disagree concerning the interpretation of this passage. The major issue centers on the identification of "the sons of God" and "the daughters of men." Three major views have been proposed.

## The Men of Rank-Common Women View

This very old view claims that "the sons of God" were human sons of powerful human aristocrats (kings, lords, nobles), and that "the daughters of men" were human daughters of common, lower classes of people. According to this view, Genesis 6:2 refers to pre-flood marriages between distinct classes of people—aristocrats and commoners.

Two arguments offered by proponents in support of this view are as follows: First, the ancient Aramaic Targums (translations of the Hebrew Old Testament in the Aramaic language) translate "sons of God" as "sons of nobles," and the Greek translation of Symmachus says "the sons of the kings or lords." Second, the Hebrew Scriptures occasionally referred to ruling judges as "gods" (elohim) [Ex. 21:6]; therefore, the sons of these judges could be called "the sons of gods."[29]

There are reasons for rejecting this view. First, this view has to draw a distinction between the daughters of men in verses 1 and 2. The word "men" in verse 1 is a generic term. It refers to all men in general; therefore, the daughters of men in verse one were the daughters of all men in general. By contrast, according to the Men of Rank-Common Women View, the daughters of men in verse 2 were not the daughters of all men in general. Instead, they were daughters of men of the lower, common classes in contrast to men of the higher, aristocratic class. The language of verses 1 and 2 does not permit such a distinction.

Second, Genesis 6:1-13 relates the human corruption of the pre-flood world and thereby explains why the flood judgment was necessary. The fact that the sons of God-daughters of men marriages are referred to at the beginning of this passage strongly implies that these marriages contributed significantly to the corruption of the human race that made the drastic flood judgment necessary. Why would marriages of sons of aristocrats to daughters of commoners contribute so significantly to the corruption of the human race? Is there something inherently corrupting in marriages between people of different classes? The Men of Rank-Common Women View seems to imply that such marriages have a more corrupting effect than aristocrat-to-aristocrat and commoner-to-commoner marriages.

Third, the biblical text implies that corruption took place as a result of *sons* of God marrying *daughters* of men. The text refers exclusively to that one kind of marriage. To remain consistent with this, the Men of Rank-Common Women View indicates that corruption took place as a result of *sons* of aristocrats marrying *daughters* of commoners. Does this mean that the marriages of *daughters* of aristocrats to *sons* of commoners would not have had a corrupting influence? If marriage between these distinctive human classes contributed significantly to corruption, why wouldn't both kinds of marriages between these classes have had the same corrupting effect?

## The Sethite Line-Cainite Line View

The second proposed view claims that "the sons of God" of Genesis 6 were human male descendants of Seth, and that "the daughters of men" were female descendants of Cain. According to this view, Genesis 6:2 refers to pre-flood marriages between two distinct lines of human descent: the godly line of Seth, recorded in Genesis 4:25-5:32, and the ungodly line of Cain, recorded in Genesis 4:1-24.

Most of the arguments offered by proponents of this view are not positive arguments in favor of their view. Instead, they are arguments against the third view, which we shall examine next.[30]

The most significant positive argument offered by some proponents is that because both the Sethite and Cainite lines of descent were recorded immediately before the Genesis 6 account of the sons of God marrying the daughters of men, it seems apparent that those lines of descent have a direct connection with the Genesis 6 marriages.

A second argument offered is the fact that the Old Testament Scriptures sometimes apply the designation "sons of God" to godly humans. C. F. Keil and Franz Delitzsch wrote:

> For it is not to angels only that the term "sons of Elohim," or "sons of Elim," is applied; but in Ps. 73:15, in an address to Elohim, the godly are called "the generation of Thy sons," i.e. sons of Elohim; in Deut. 32:5 the Israelites are called His (God's) sons, and in Hos. 1:10, "sons of the living God;" and in Ps. 80:17, Israel is spoken of as the son, whom Elohim has made strong.[31]

There are reasons for rejecting this view. First, the word "men" in Genesis 6:1-2, 4 is a generic term. Evidence for this is seen in the fact that the Hebrew noun translated "men" in these verses is singular in number (literal translation, *the man*), but the pronoun "them" at the end of verse 1, which refers back to that noun, is plural. This indicates that in these verses the noun "men" is referring to all mankind in general. Thus, "the daughters of men" in these verses were female descendants of all mankind, not of one specific line distinct from the rest of mankind. This means that the "daughters of men" whom "the sons of God" married (vv. 2, 4) were female descendants of all mankind, not exclusively of the Cainite line. By contrast, the Sethite Line-Cainite Line View identifies them as female descendants of just the Cainite line.

Second, as noted with the first view, the biblical text of Genesis 6 implies that corruption took place as a result of *sons* of God marrying *daughters* of men. The text refers exclusively to that one kind of marriage. To remain consistent with this, the Sethite Line-Cainite Line View indicates that corruption took place as a result of *sons* of the Sethite line marrying *daughters* of the Cainite line. Does this mean that the marriage of *daughters* of the Sethite line to *sons* of the Cainite line would not have had a corrupting influence? If it were marriage between these two human lines that contributed significantly to corruption, why wouldn't both kinds of marriages between these two lines have had the same corrupting effect? It is unlikely that marriage between the two lines would have been exclusively that of Sethite men marrying Cainite women, but no Sethite women marrying Cainite men.

Third, it is interesting to note that the Sethite Line-Cainite Line View did not begin until the fourth century A.D. This makes it the newest of the three major views. The *New Catholic Encyclopedia* states that this view "that sees in these sons of God the Sethites and in the daughters of men the Cainites dates from the 4th century and is influenced by theological concern for maintaining the spirituality of the angels."[32] This seems to imply that the major motivation for starting this view was not exegesis of Scripture but opposition to the

Angel View that we shall examine next.

## The Fallen Angel-Human Women View

The third proposed view claims that "the sons of God" of Genesis 6 were fallen angels and that "the daughters of men" were human women in general. According to this view, Genesis 6:1-2, 4 recorded the following situation: A group of fallen angels left the domain of angels and deserted their dwelling place in the first heaven to become part of the domain of mankind and to make the earth their dwelling place. They then married human women, entered into sexual relationships with them, and thereby fathered children who were the mighty men of renown of the pre-flood world. The Hebrew words that describe these offspring (v. 4) indicate that they were "the heroes or champions," successful warriors, famous for their great "strength and vitality."[33]

**Problems and Answers**: Opponents of this view point out its problems. First, as we saw in an earlier chapter, because angels are spirit beings by nature, they do not have physical bodies of flesh and bones and are sexless. How, then, could they have sexual relationships with human women and beget children?

This is, perhaps, the greatest problem with the Angel View. However, in that same chapter we also saw that although it is true that angels by nature do not have physical bodies and are sexless, there have been instances in which some have temporarily taken on physical bodies that could be seen and touched. We noted an example of this in Genesis 18-19. Two angels who appeared in male human form had physical bodies that could eat food, physical feet that could be washed, and physical hands that could touch. The men of Sodom and Gomorrah identified them as men.

In light of this biblical incident and the fact that the Bible does not reveal how or where those angels got the bodies, we should be cautious about quickly concluding that because angels by nature do not have physical bodies and are sexless, the Angel View proposes something impossible. In conjunction with this, Merrill F. Unger wrote, "To deny such a possibility...is to assume, it would seem, a degree of knowledge of fallen angelic nature which man does not possess."[34]

A second problem for the Angel View proposed by opponents is Jesus' teaching that angels do not marry (Mk. 12:25). By contrast, the Angel View asserts that fallen angels married human women. Doesn't that view contradict Jesus' clear teaching?

In response to this problem, it should be noted that Jesus taught that the angels "who are in heaven" (lit., *in the heavens*) do not marry. By contrast, the Angel View does not assert that it was angels in the heavens who married. Instead, it claims that it was angels who deserted the heavens and came to earth who married.

A third proposed problem is that the personal beings of Jude 7 engaged in fornication, but the sons of God of Genesis 6 contracted marriages. Opponents of the Angel View argue that fornication and marriage are not the same; therefore, the sons of God of Genesis 6 cannot be the personal beings of Jude 7.

The response to this argument is twofold. First, as noted earlier, sometimes the term *fornication* refers to any kind of sexual relationship forbidden by God. Because angels by nature are sexless, it is apparent that God never intended angels to have sexual relationships. Thus, any sexual relationship of angels with human women would be forbidden by God and could be called fornication.

Second, although contracting marriages between angels and human women may have been recognized as legitimate by the ancient world, that did not guarantee the same recognition by God. Because God would have been opposed to sexual relationships between angels and human women, surely He would have regarded these marriages as illegitimate or forbidden. In other words, according to God's values, these angels and human women were not genuinely married. Instead, they were living together in fornication.

A fourth argument offered by critics is that the Fallen Angel-Human Women View is based on pagan mythology, not biblical revelation. According to Babylonian and Greek mythology, in ancient times gods came to earth in male human form, had sexual relationships with human women, and thereby begot half divine-half human children who became great heroes through their superhuman feats.[35] Critics assert that the Fallen Angel-Human Women View was developed as a result of its proponents allowing this pagan mythology to determine their interpretation of Genesis 6.

The response to this argument is that instead of the Fallen Angel-Human Women View being a perversion of Genesis 6 based upon pagan mythology, it is more likely that the pagan mythology is a perversion of the actual events that are recorded in Genesis 6.[36] The Babylonian Gilgamesh Epic and other pagan stories of the great flood that destroyed the ancient world are examples of perverted accounts of the actual flood recorded in Genesis 6-8.

**Reasons for Acceptance**: There are good reasons for accepting the Fallen Angel-Human Women View as the correct view. First, the New Testament passages 2 Peter 2:4 and Jude 6-7, which we examined earlier, require this understanding of Genesis 6. If "the sons of God" who married "the daughters of men" were not fallen angels, then when did the angels in 2 Peter 2:4 and Jude 6-7 leave the domain of angels to become part of another domain that God did not intend for angels? When did they desert their dwelling place in the first heaven to live in another location? When did these angels give themselves over to forbidden sexual relationships? When did they pursue flesh that God intended to be foreign to them? When did these angels commit a sin that was so serious that God imprisoned them in Tartarus, confining them there until their final judgment at the end of history?

Proponents of the other views of Genesis 6 claim that 2 Peter 2:4 and Jude 6 refer to the original sin of angelic rebellion.[37] However, as noted earlier, if this were true, all fallen angels— including Satan—would have been imprisoned in Tartarus in ancient times. Instead, the Scriptures clearly indicate that Satan and his host of demons are still free and active in the universe.

Second, as noted earlier, the "men" in Genesis 6:1-2, 4 is generic, referring to all mankind in general rather than to one specific class or line of men. Thus, "daughters of men" were female descendants of all mankind in general, rather than of one specific class or line of men. The Fallen Angel-Human Women View is the only view that agrees with this. The other views claim that "the daughters of men" are female descendants of one specific class or line of men.

Third, the historic understanding of the Jews, going back at least to the second century before Christ and perhaps earlier, was that "the sons of God" of Genesis 6 were angels who came from the heavens to earth, married human women, and fathered abnormal children who corrupted the world so much that it became necessary for God to send the flood to destroy this perversion of humanity. God had these angels bound in the depths of the earth, separate from other beings. They will be kept there until their eternal judgment at the end of history.

Several pieces of ancient Jewish literature express this view. The dates of this literature demonstrate the fact that the Fallen Angel-Human Women View is the oldest view concerning Genesis 6.

The Septuagint, the Greek translation of the Hebrew Old Testament, produced by Jewish scholars beginning in the third or second centuries before Christ, indicated that "the sons of God" of Genesis 6 were angels.[38]

*The Book of Enoch* and *The Book of Jubilees*, Jewish literature produced in the third or second centuries before Christ, presented the same view. *The Book of Enoch* stated,

And the angels, the children of the heaven, saw and lusted after them, and said to one another: "Come, let us choose us wives from among the children of men and beget us children."

And they have gone to the daughters of men upon the earth, and have slept with the women, and have defiled themselves, and revealed to them all kinds of sins. And the women have borne giants, and the whole earth has thereby been filled with blood and unrighteousness.[39]

Concerning these angels, *The Book of Jubilees* asserted,

And after this they were bound in the depths of the earth forever, until the day of the great condemnation, when judgment is executed on all those who have corrupted their ways and works before the Lord.

For owing to these three things came the flood upon the earth, namely, owing to the fornication wherein the Watchers against the law of their ordinances went a whoring after the daughters of men, and took to themselves wives of all which they chose: and they made the beginning of uncleanness. And they begat sons the Naphidim, and they were all unlike, and they devoured one another.[40]

Josephus, the famous Jewish historian of the first century A.D., wrote,

For many angels of God companied with women, and begat sons that proved unjust, and despisers of all that was good on account of the confidence they had in their own strength; For the tradition is, that these men did what resembled the acts of those whom the Grecians called *giants.*[41]

It is interesting to note that Jude, who in verses 6-7 wrote about angels who had sexual relationships with human women, quoted from *The Book of Enoch* later in his book (Jude 14-15).

Fourth, the historic view of the early church until the fourth century A.D. was that "the sons of God" of Genesis 6 were fallen angels who married human women and fathered unique children through them. Several expressions by early church leaders demonstrate this.

Justin Martyr (114-165 A.D.), a significant early apologist for Christianity against paganism and Judaism, wrote, "But the angels transgressed this appointment, and were captivated by love of women, and begat children." He claimed that ancient poets and mythologists mistakenly ascribed this angelic activity to gods.[42]

Irenaeus (120-202 A.D.), Bishop of Lyons and disciple of Polycarp, who had been taught by the Apostle John, stated, "And in the days of Noah He justly brought on the deluge for the purpose of extinguishing that most infamous race of men then existent, who could not bring forth fruit to God, since the angels that sinned had commingled with them."[43]

Tertullian (145-220 A.D.), Latin church leader and apologist, referred to "those angels, to wit, who rushed from heaven on the daughters of men," to "women who possessed angels (as husbands)," and to the angels who repudiated heaven and engaged in "carnal marriage."[44]

Lactantius (240-320 A.D.), Christian apologist and very learned teacher of Emperor Constantine's son, declared that angels from heaven had intercourse with women on earth and fathered children with a mixed angelic-human nature.[45]

Fifth, Babylonian, Greek, and other mythology taught that in ancient times gods came to earth from the heavens in male human form, married human women, and fathered superhuman children who became famous. We certainly do not base theology upon pagan mythology, but we must ask what prompted this mythological concept. Surely marriage between human men and women born on the earth would not have prompted the concept of super-natural beings coming from the heavens in male human form, marrying human women, and fathering superhuman children.

The combination of the teaching of 2 Peter 2:4 and Jude 6-7, the generic term "men" in Genesis 6:1-2, 4, and the consistent understanding of ancient Judaism and the early church prompts the conclusion that the Fallen Angel-Human Women View of Genesis 6 relates what actually happened in the pre-flood world. Through time pagan people perverted the account of what actually happened. For example, they misinterpreted the angels as gods. This pagan mythological concept is a perverted response to what actually happened and thereby is an inference in favor of the Fallen Angel-Human Women View of Genesis 6.

Sixth, Genesis 6:9-10 states, "These are the generations of Noah: Noah was a just man and perfect in his generations, and Noah walked with God. And Noah begot three sons, Shem, Ham, and Japheth." The word translated "generations" basically means *descendants*. It comes from a term that "in its narrowest sense describes the act of a woman in giving birth to a child, but it is sometimes used of the father's part in becoming a parent." [46] The meaning of this term plus the statement in verse 10 about Noah begetting three sons indicates that this passage is talking about Noah's physical descendants.

Verse 9 declares that Noah was "perfect" in his descendants. This cannot mean that his physical descendants were sinlessly perfect because no humans born through natural means since the fall of man are sinlessly perfect. The word translated "perfect" means "sound, wholesome, unimpaired."[47] It sometimes was used to describe unblemished animals.[48] Thus, this passage declares that Noah's physical descendants were sound, whole-some, or unimpaired. The descendants of "the sons of God" of Genesis 6 were not sound, wholesome, or unimpaired. They were blemished with a fallen angelic strain. Noah's descendants were not blemished with that strain. They were completely human as intended by God.

Seventh, the Genesis 6 record implies that the marriages of the sons of God to the daughters of men contributed significantly to the corruption of the human race that made the drastic worldwide judgment of the flood necessary. If these marriages were between two different classes or lines of human beings, why did God bring this worldwide judgment thousands of years before the final worldwide judgment at the end of this earth's history? Ever since the flood judgment, marriages between different classes and lines of human beings have taken place, but God withholds another worldwide judgment until the end of history.

This difference in worldwide judgment strongly implies that the marriages of the sons of God with the daughters of men in Genesis 6 were not between two different classes or lines of human beings. They must have been marriages between human beings and beings of another order—marriages that mixed together two radically different natures, thereby producing such a radical perversion of what God had created that worldwide judgment became necessary to prevent this radical perversion from spreading to all mankind.

In line with this conclusion, Merrill F. Unger wrote concerning the marriages in Genesis 6,

> The divine account in the Old Testament and the inspired comments in the New Testament unanimously represent the whole episode as being a unique and shocking abnormality, breaking down every God-ordained law for both the physical and the spiritual realms, and producing outrageous confusion in both; so that the unmitigated incarceration in the lowest pits of Tartarus is the penalty for the angelic offenders on the one hand, and a world-engulfing deluge the punishment for human

folly on the other.[49]

The time and drastic nature of the worldwide flood judgment favor the validity of the Fallen Angel-Human Women View.

## A Possible Satanic Strategy

Immediately after the fall of man, God told Satan that the woman's seed would crush him (Gen. 3:15). Through further revelation, God indicated what He meant by that statement. During the course of world history, a man-child Redeemer would be born of a woman into the world. While in the world, the Redeemer would do the work of redemption through which Satan would be crushed. Thus, the Redeemer would be the key to God's defeating Satan before the history of this world ends.

Since the Redeemer would be the key to God's defeating him, Satan drew the following conclusion: If he could prevent the Redeemer from being born into the world, God would never defeat him. As a result of this conclusion, Satan's goal throughout the course of post-fall, Old Testament history was to prevent the Redeemer from being born into the world.

Satan tried many different means to accomplish this goal.[50] It may be that one of those means was the marriage of fallen angels to human women. The Redeemer's work of redemption, through which Satan will be crushed, provides salvation for fallen human beings, but it does not provide salvation for fallen angels. Because God does not provide salvation for fallen angels, if Satan could introduce a fallen angelic strain into the human race and then have that strain permeate the entire race before the Redeemer was born, that would destroy the whole redemptive program of God. It would render useless the birth of the Redeemer into the world because there would be no beings completely human in nature left to redeem.

The assumption that this was Satan's strategy prompts the conclusion that the spread of this fallen angelic strain, generation after generation, through the process of marriages and procreation had to be stopped for the sake of God's redemptive program. Thus, while there was at least one man left whose descendants were completely human—not blemished with the angelic strain—God destroyed the mixed multitude with the worldwide flood but preserved Noah and his family through the ark.

## 1 Peter 3:18-20

A passage that seems to be related to this concept of a possible Satanic strategy is 1 Peter 3:18-20, which says,

> For Christ also hath once suffered for sins, the just for the unjust, that he might bring us to God, being put to death in the flesh, but made alive by the Spirit, By whom also he went and preached unto the spirits in prison, Who at one time were disobedient, when once the long-suffering of God waited in the days of Noah, while the ark was preparing.

Three major interpretations have been proposed for this passage. First, during the days of Noah before the flood, Christ preached through him to the unsaved, disobedient people of the world, who later perished in the flood and whose disembodied spirits are now imprisoned in hell. Second, after His death on the cross, Christ descended into hell to preach to the imprisoned, disembodied spirits of the unsaved, disobedient people of Noah's days who perished in the flood. Third, after His death on the cross, Christ descended into Tartarus to make a proclamation to the imprisoned sons of God of Genesis 6—the fallen angels who married human women in the days of Noah before the flood.[51]

The majority of scholars today advocate the third or Fallen Angel View.[52] The language of verses 19 and 20 seems to indicate that Christ's preaching took place at a different time than the disobedience in the days of Noah.[53] This militates against the first view of Christ's preaching through Noah during the days before the flood.

Second, when the word "spirit" is used without a qualifying phrase, as it is in 1 Peter 3:19, it normally refers to supernatural spirit beings, not humans or human spirits.[54] By contrast, Sydney H. T. Page indicates that when the word refers to a human spirit, it is used with a qualifying phrase, and thereby "the person is represented as *having* a spirit rather than *being* a spirit."[55] Page further states,

> This is true even in Hebrews 12:23, which mentions "the spirits of righteous men made perfect." Here the qualifying phrase "of righteous men made perfect" indicates that the spirits belong to human beings. If Peter had intended to refer to people in 1 Peter 3:19, he likely would have written, based on New Testament usage, a phrase such as "the spirits of those who were disobedient."[56]

This refutes the first and second views, which have Christ preaching to humans or human spirits.

Page presents a third reason for advocating the Fallen Angel View.

> It is found in the close relationship between 1 Peter 3:19-20 and 2 Peter 2:4. The latter speaks of God's judgment on fallen angels and exhibits a number of parallels to the former. Where 1 Peter speaks of disobedient spirits, 2 Peter speaks of angels who sinned, but the two accounts are so similar that they are likely referring to the same episode. In both cases, we find the idea of perpetrators of sin who are incarcerated, and in both, this is mentioned in the context of a reference to Noah and the flood. It is difficult to believe that these similarities are simply coincidental.[57]

Page's statements imply that because 2 Peter 2:4 refers to fallen angels, the disobedient spirits of 1 Peter 3:19-20 must also be a reference to the same fallen angels. In addition, because both passages present their statements in the context of a reference to Noah and the flood, both must be referring to angels who were disobedient during the days of Noah before the flood.

Fourth, the angel view gives excellent insight concerning why Peter wrote 3:18-20 at this point in his letter. Immediately before this passage he referred to persecution confronting his readers (3:13-17), and later he made it clear that Satan's forces were the ultimate instigators of this persecution (5:8-9). With this in mind, Peter wrote 3:18-20 to encourage his persecuted readers with the fact that Christ had gained a tremendous victory over Satan's forces through His work of redemption on the cross. Thus, in 3:22 he wrote that Christ "is gone into heaven, and is on the right hand of God, angels and authorities and powers being made subject unto him."[58]

For these reasons, I believe that the Fallen Angel View is the correct interpretation of 1 Peter 3:18-20. But, if this understanding is correct, why did Christ go to this specific group of fallen angels to make a proclamation after His death on the cross? And what did He proclaim to them?

Perhaps Christ went to this specific group of fallen angels because of what they did in the days of Noah before the flood. They married human women to introduce a fallen angelic strain into the human race, a strain that they hoped would eventually permeate the entire race and thereby prevent the Redeemer from coming into the world and doing the work of redemption through which Satan would be crushed. After Christ died on the cross, He went to this group of angels imprisoned in Tartarus to proclaim that He was the Redeemer, that He had just completed the work of redemption through His death on the cross, that their scheme therefore had failed, and their future judgment was certain. Similarly, Page asserted that Christ's preaching was His "declaration to the wicked angels of his triumph over them,"[59] and Blum said that it was Christ's announcement "of his victory and of their doom."[60]

# ENDNOTES

[1] Holladay, *Concise Hebrew and Aramaic Lexicon*; quoted by Ralph H. Alexander, "Ezekiel," in *The Expositor's Bible Commentary*, Vol. 6, ed. by Frank E. Gaebelein (Grand Rapids: Zondervan Publishing House, 1986), p. 885.

[2] J. Barton Payne, "tamim," *Theological Wordbook of the Old Testament*, Vol. II, ed. by R. Laird Harris, Gleason L. Archer, Jr., and Bruce K. Waltke (Chicago: Moody Press, 1980), p. 974.

[3] G. Herbert Livingston, "awel, awla," *Theological Wordbook of the Old Testament*, Vol. II, p. 653.

[4] Gerhard von Rad, "ouranos," *Theological Dictionary of the New Testament*, Vol. V, ed. by Gerhard Friedrich, trans. and ed. by Geoffrey W. Bromiley (Grand Rapids: Wm. B. Eerdmans Publishing Company, 1967), p. 505, text plus footnote 63.

[5] Friedrich Lang, "pur," *Theological Dictionary of the New Testament*, Vol. VI, ed. by Gerhard Friedrich, trans. and ed. by Geoffrey W. Bromiley (Grand Rapids: Wm. B. Eerdmans Publishing Company, 1968), p. 936.

[6] Francis Brown, S.R. Driver, and Charles A. Briggs, *A Hebrew and English Lexicon of the Old Testament* (Oxford: Clarendon Press, 1975), p. 237.

[7] Leonard J. Coppes, "helel," *Theological Wordbook of the Old Testament*, Vol. I, ed. by R. Laird Harris, Gleason L. Archer, Jr., and Bruce K. Waltke (Chicago: Moody Press, 1980), p. 217.

[8] Brown, Driver, and Briggs, *A Hebrew and English Lexicon of the Old Testament*, p. 237.

[9] Victor P. Hamilton, "shahar," *Theological Wordbook of the Old Testament*, Vol. II, ed. by R. Laird Harris, Gleason L. Archer, Jr.,

and Bruce K. Waltke (Chicago: Moody Press, 1980), p. 917.

[10] William F. Arndt and F. Wilbur Gingrich, *A Greek-English Lexicon of the New Testament* (Chicago: The University of Chicago Press, 1957), p. 839.

[11] Henry Alford, *The Greek Testament*, Vol. I (Chicago: Moody Press, 1958), p. 540.

[12] William F. Arndt and F. Wilbur Gingrich, *A Greek-English Lexicon of the New Testament*, p. 752.

[13] *Ibid.,* p. 446.

[14] A. Skevington Wood, "Ephesians," *The Expositor's Bible Commentary*, Vol. 11, p. 86.

[15] E. K. Simpson, *Commentary on the Epistle to the Ephesians* in *The New International Commentary on the New Testament*, ed. by F. F. Bruce (Grand Rapids: Wm. B. Eerdmans Publishing Company, 1975), p. 143.

[16] Geoffrey W. Grogan, "Isaiah," *The Expositor's Bible Commentary*, Vol. 6, p. 105.

[17] Robert L. Thomas, *Revelation 8-22* (Chicago: Moody Press, 1995), p. 124.

[18] Werner Foerster, "daimon," *Theological Dictionary of the New Testament,* Vol. II, ed. by Gerhard Kittel, trans. and ed. by Geoffrey W. Bromiley (Grand Rapids: Wm. B. Eerdmans Publishing Company, 1964), p. 18.

[19] William F. Arndt and F. Wilbur Gingrich, *A Greek-English Lexicon of the New Testament*, p. 813.

[20] R. H. Strachan, "The Second Epistle General of Peter," in *The Expositor's Greek Testament*, Vol. V, ed. by W. Robertson Nicoll (Grand Rapids: Wm. B. Eerdmans Publishing Company, n.d.), pp. 134-35.

[21] Joachim Jeremias, "abussos," *Theological Dictionary of the New Testament*, Vol. I, ed. by Gerhard Kittel, trans. and ed. by

Geoffrey W. Bromiley (Grand Rapids: Wm. B. Eerdmans Publishing Company, 1964), p. 9.

[22] Merrill F. Unger, *Biblical Demonology* (Wheaton, IL: Scripture Press, 1952), p. 53.

[23] William F. Arndt and F. Wilbur Gingrich, *A Greek-English Lexicon of the New Testament*, p. 112.

[24] Otto Michel, "oiketerion," *Theological Dictionary of the New Testament*, Vol. V, ed. by Gerhard Friedrich, trans. and ed. by Geoffrey W. Bromiley (Grand Rapids: Wm. B. Eerdmans Publishing Company, 1967), p. 155.

[25] Walter C. Kaiser, Jr., *More Hard Sayings of the Old Testament* (Downers Grove, IL: InterVarsity Press, 1992), p. 35.

[26] Edwin A. Blum, "Jude," *The Expositor's Bible Commentary*, Vol. 12, p. 390.

[27] William F. Arndt and F. Wilbur Gingrich, *A Greek-English Lexicon of the New Testament*, p. 699.

[28] *Ibid.*, p. 578.

[29] Walter C. Kaiser, Jr., *More Hard Sayings of the Old Testament*, p. 37.

[30] For an example of this, see C. F. Keil and Franz Delitzsch, *The Pentateuch*, Vol. I, in *Biblical Commentary on the Old Testament* (Grand Rapids: Wm B. Eerdmans Publishing Company, 1959), pp. 127-35.

[31] *Ibid.,* p. 128.

[32] "Sons of God," *New Catholic Encyclopedia*, Vol. XIII (New York: McGraw-Hill Book Company), p. 435.

[33] John N. Oswalt, "gibbor," *Theological Wordbook of the Old Testament,* Vol. I, pp. 148-49.

[34] Merrill F. Unger, *Biblical Demonology*, p. 50.

[35] William Foxwell Albright, *From the Stone Age to Christianity* (Baltimore: Johns Hopkins Press, 1940), p. 226.

[36] Franz Delitzsch, *Genesis*, in Lange's *A Commentary on the Holy Scriptures* (New York: Charles Scribner's Sons, 1865), p. 284.

[37] Walter C. Kaiser, Jr., *More Hard Sayings of the Old Testament*, p. 35.

[38] "Sons of God," *New Catholic Encyclopedia*, Vol. XIII, p. 435.

[39] R. H. Charles, *The Book of Enoch* (Oxford: The Clarendon Press, 1912), pp. 14-15, 21.

[40] R. H. Charles, *The Book of Jubilees* (New York: The Macmillan Company, 1917), pp. 57-58, 68.

[41] Flavius Josephus, *Antiquities of the Jews*, Vol. I, Chpt. 3, in *The Complete Works of Flavius Josephus*, trans. by William Whiston (Chicago: Thompson & Thomas, n.d.), p. 32.

[42] Justin Martyr, "The Second Apology of Justin," Chpt. V, in *Ante-Nicene Fathers*, Vol. 1, ed. by Alexander Roberts and James Donaldson (Peabody, MA: Hendrickson Publishers, 1994), p. 190.

[43] Irenaeus, *Against Heresies*, Book IV, Chpt. XXXVI, Sec. 4, in *The Ante-Nicene Fathers*, Vol. 1, p. 516.

[44] Quintus Septimius Florens Tertullian, "On the Apparel of Women," Book I, chpts. II and IV, in *Ante-Nicene Fathers*, Vol. 4, pp. 14-16.

[45] Lucius Caecilius Firmianus Lactantius, *The Divine Institutes*, Book II, Chpt. XV, in *Ante-Nicene Fathers*, Vol. 7, p. 64.

[46] Paul R. Gilchrist, "toledot," *Theological Wordbook of the Old Testament*, Vol. I, p. 378.

[47] Brown, Driver, and Briggs, *A Hebrew and English Lexicon of the New Testament*, p. 1071.

[48] J. Barton Payne, "tamim," *Theological Wordbook of the Old Testament* Vol. II, p. 974.

[49] Merrill F. Unger, *Biblical Demonology*, p. 51.

[50] For a study of these means see Renald E. Showers, *What on Earth is God Doing?* (Neptune, NJ: Loizeaux Brothers, 1973).

[51] Edwin A. Blum, "1 Peter," in *The Expositor's Bible Commentary*, Vol. 12, ed. by Frank E. Gaebelein (Grand Rapids: Zondervan Publishing House, 1981), p. 241.

[52] Gerhard Friedrich, "kerusso," *Theological Dictionary of the New Testament*, Vol. III, ed. by Gerhard Kittel, trans. and ed. by Geoffrey W. Bromiley (Grand Rapids: Wm. B. Eerdmans Publishing Company, 1965), p. 707.

[53] *Ibid.*

[54] Roger M. Raymer, "1 Peter," *The Bible Knowledge Commentary*, New Testament edition, ed. by John F. Walvoord and Roy B. Zuck (Wheaton, IL: Victor Books, 1983), p. 851.

[55] Sydney H. T. Page, *Powers of Evil* (Grand Rapids: Baker Books, 1995), p. 231.

[56] *Ibid.*

[57] *Ibid.*, p. 232.

[58] *Ibid.*, pp. 232-33.

[59] *Ibid.*, p. 235.

[60] Edwin A. Blum, "1 Peter," *The Expositor's Bible Commentary*, Vol. 12, p. 242.

## 6

# NO SALVATION FOR
# FALLEN ANGELS

### The Relationship of Salvation to Holy Angels

Because the holy angels have never sinned and, as noted earlier, are now confirmed or locked into a permanent sinless state, we can conclude that they have no need for salvation. The question in Hebrews 1:14, which indicates that the holy angels are "all ministering spirits, sent forth to minister for them who shall be heirs of salvation," substantiates this conclusion. It signifies that the holy angels are distinct from the heirs of salvation.

### The Relationship of Salvation to Fallen Angels

Two biblical passages indicate that God does not provide salvation for fallen angels.

**Hebrews 2:14-16**: After declaring that Christ, as the captain of the salvation of human beings, was made a little lower than the angels in His incarnation (2:9-10), the writer of Hebrews wrote concerning Him,

> Forasmuch, then, as the children are partakers of flesh and blood, he also himself likewise took part of the same, that through death he might destroy him that had the power of death, that is, the devil, And deliver them who, through fear of death, were all their lifetime subject to bondage. For verily he took not on him the nature of angels, but he took on him the seed of Abraham.

Through these statements, the writer of Hebrews indicated that to provide salvation for fallen human beings, Christ in His incarnation took upon Himself a complete human nature and died as the substitute for human beings. Thus, the only way that salvation could be provided for fallen human beings was by Christ becoming human.

These statements in Hebrews imply that the only way salvation can be provided for fallen beings is by the Savior taking upon Himself the nature of those beings. He must become the same kind of being as they. In light of this implication, the statement that Christ did not take upon Himself the nature of angels (v. 16) is very significant. It signifies that Christ did not become an angel, and salvation therefore is not provided for fallen angels.

**1 Peter 1:12**: After referring to the salvation of human souls (v. 9) and the things that pertain to that salvation (vv. 10-12), Peter made the following statement at the end of verse 12: "which things the angels desire to look into."

Edwin A. Blum states that the word translated "to look into" means " 'to stoop over to look.' It implies willingness to exert or inconvenience oneself to obtain a better perspective. Here the present tense gives it a continuous aspect."[1]

From this definition, we can conclude that Peter was saying that angels have such an intense desire to learn about the salvation of fallen human beings that they are continuously willing to exert or inconvenience themselves to study it. The salvation of fallen human beings is an intriguing mystery to them because they themselves can never personally experience salvation.

Peter's statement prompted Henry Alford to write, "It enhances further still the excellence of the salvation revealed to us, that angels, for whom it is not designed as for us (Heb. 2:16), long to pry into its mysteries."[2]

Alford also quoted Hoffman (Schriftb. i. 313) as saying,

> Angels have only the contrast between good and evil, without the power of conversion from sin to righteousness. Being then witnesses of such conversion to God, they long to penetrate the knowledge of the means by which it is brought about.... They themselves are placed outside the scheme of salvation: therefore it is said that they desire to look into the facts of the apostolic preaching.[3]

## The Great Contrast

God has provided salvation for fallen human beings but not for fallen angels. At this point only He knows the reason for this great contrast. Perhaps it was because angels were created with greater intelligence and were exposed to greater revelation than human beings before their fall and therefore sinned against greater light.

Regardless of the reason, we human beings who have received God's gift of salvation through faith in His Son Jesus Christ should thank God profusely for His grace, which prompted Him to provide salvation for us, in spite of the fact that we too had rebelled against Him.

Many years ago, John R. Sweney and Johnson Oatman, Jr. wrote the following hymn that expresses this great contrast in poetic form:

### Holy, Holy, Is What the Angels Sing

There is singing up in heaven such as we have never known, Where the angels sing the praises of the Lamb upon the throne; Their sweet harps are ever tuneful and their voices always clear, O that we might be more like them while we serve the Master here!

But I hear another anthem, blending voices clear and strong, "Unto Him who hath redeemed us and hath bought us," is the song; We have come thro' tribulations to this land so fair and bright, In the fountain freely flowing He hath made our garments white.

Then the angels stand and listen, for they cannot join that song, Like the sound of many waters, by that happy, blood-washed throng; For they sing about great trials, battles fought and vict'ries won, And they praise their great Redeemer, who hath said to them, "Well done."

So, although I'm not an angel, yet I know that over there I will join a blessed chorus that the angels cannot share; I will sing about my Saviour, who upon dark Calvary freely pardoned my transgressions, died to set a sinner free.

CHORUS

Holy, holy, is what the angels sing,  And I expect to help them make the courts of heaven ring; But when I sing redemption's story, they will fold their wings, For angels never felt the joys that our salvation brings.

## ENDNOTES

[1] Edwin A. Blum, "1 Peter," *The Expositor's Bible Commentary*,

Vol. 12, ed. by Frank E. Gaebelein (Grand Rapids: Zondervan Publishing House, 1981), p. 222.

[2] Henry Alford, "1 Peter," in *The Greek Testament*, Vol. IV (Chicago: Moody Press, 1958), p. 338.

[3] *Ibid.*

7

---

# THE DWELLING PLACES
# AND JUDGMENTS OF
# ANGELS

---

### The Dwelling Place of the Holy Angels

G od created all of the angels as sinless, holy beings. Their dwelling place was the heaven in which God dwells in a special sense—the heaven that the Apostle Paul called "the third heaven" (2 Cor. 12:2). Those angels who later chose to remain loyal to God and, as a result, were confirmed forever in their holy state continue to dwell in that heaven.

Several things indicate that the holy angels have the third heaven as their dwelling place. For example, the Apostle John saw an enormous host of holy angels around the throne of God in that heaven (Rev. 5:11-13). Jesus referred to the angels in heaven who behold the face of God there (Mt. 18:10). The angel Gabriel stands in the presence of God and was sent from God to the virgin Mary in the city of Nazareth (Lk. 1:19, 26). A holy angel came from heaven to strengthen Jesus during His Gethsemane agony (Lk. 22:43). John saw seven angels who stand before God (Rev. 8:2). In conjunction with the Second Coming of Christ, a holy angel will come down from heaven to imprison Satan in the bottomless pit (Rev. 20:1-3).

Several of these examples indicate that although the holy angels dwell in God's third heaven, they are not confined there. Holy angels have accesss to the earth to perform God-assigned tasks.

## The Dwelling Places and Judgments of the Fallen, Evil Angels

When Satan and the other evil angels rebelled against God and thereby fell away from Him and their original holy state, they were cast from God's third heaven down to the first heaven in the vicinity of the earth. Thus, their initial judgment because of their original rebellion changed their dwelling place from God's third heaven to the first heaven.

The fallen, evil angels are now subdivided into two groups: the fallen, confined angels and the fallen, free angels. We saw that the fallen, confined angels were subjected to an additional stage of judgment because they abandoned their dwelling place in the first heaven to dwell on earth and marry human women during the days of Noah before the flood. God judged them by imprisoning them in Tartarus (the abyss or bottomless pit) until the great day of judgment. As a result, Tartarus continues to be the dwelling place of those evil angels. They are not free to leave the abyss.

The fallen, free angels did not abandon their dwelling place in the first heaven to dwell on earth and marry human women. As a result, the first heaven continues to be their dwelling place. Paul therefore called them "the power of the air" (Eph. 2:2), and Gerhard Delling stated that "their abode is now...the lowest of the different heavenly spheres."[1] We noted in an earlier chapter that although the first heaven is the dwelling place of these fallen angels, they are free to come to earth as demons to do Satan's work. Satan, as their ruler, also continues to dwell in the first heaven (Eph. 2:2), but he also has access to God's third heaven and the earth (Job 1:6-7).

An additional stage in the judgment of Satan and the fallen, free angels will take place in the middle of the seven-year Tribulation period. At that time they will be cast down from the first heaven to the earth (Rev. 12:7-12). As a result, the earth will be their dwelling place for three and one-half years (the second half of the Tribulation period; Rev. 12:13-17; cp. vv. 4-6).

Satan and the fallen, free angels will be removed from earth and imprisoned in Tartarus in conjunction with the Second Coming of Christ after the Tribulation (Rev. 20:1-3; Isa. 24:21-23). The Revelation 20 passage refers to the chaining and imprisonment of Satan in the bottomless pit in conjunction with Christ's coming, and the Isaiah 24 passage states, "And it shall come to pass in that day, that the LORD shall punish the host of the high ones that are on high...And they shall be gathered together, as prisoners are gathered in the pit, and shall be shut up in the prison." Concerning this passage, Franz Delitzsch asserted that the host on high refers to angels, that God will judge them by thrusting them "from above downwards into the pit and prison," that the pit is the same place of angelic imprisonment referred to in 2 Peter 2:4 and Jude 6, and that this passage has a parallel in Revelation 20:1-3.[2]

Through this additional stage in their judgment, Satan and the fallen, free angels will enter the same pit of gloom where the angels of Genesis 6 who married human women have been imprisoned since the Noahic flood. Thus, Satan and all the fallen angels will have Tartarus as their dwelling place, and they will remain imprisoned there throughout the thousand-year millennial reign of Christ and His saints on the earth (Rev. 20:2-6). In line with this, Isaiah 24:22-23 indicates that the fallen angels will be in this prison for "many days" while the Lord reigns on the earth.

After the Millennium, Satan will be loosed from his prison in Tartarus (Rev. 20:7). He will return to the earth to lead a final revolt against the rule of Christ and the saints, but God will crush that revolt quickly (Rev. 20:8-9).

Then Satan will be removed from the earth and cast forever into the lake of fire and brimstone (Rev. 20:10). At that time, all of the fallen angels will be cast forever into that same lake of fire. Concerning the fallen angels, Isaiah 24:22 states that after they have been in the pit (Tartarus) many days (the days of the Millennium), they shall "be visited." Franz Delitzsch indicates that this refers to a visitation of divine wrath, the "infliction of the final punishment" on fallen angels described as "the judgment of the great day" in Jude 6 (see also 2 Pet. 2:4).[3] Thus, through this final stage of their judgment, Satan and all the fallen angels will have the lake of fire and brimstone as their eternal dwelling place. There they will "be tormented day and night forever and ever" (Rev. 20:10). In line with this, Christ referred to the "everlasting fire, prepared for the devil and his angels" (Mt. 25:41).

## ENDNOTES

[1] Gerhard Delling, "arche," *Theological Dictionary of the New Testament*, Vol. I, ed. by Gerhard Kittel, trans. and ed. by Geoffrey W. Bromiley (Grand Rapids: Wm. B. Eerdmans Publishing Company, 1964), p. 483.

[2] Franz Delitzsch, *Biblical Commentary on the Prophecies of*

*Isaiah*, Vol. I, trans. by James Martin (Grand Rapids: Wm. B. Eerdmans Publishing Company, 1960), pp. 434-35.

[3] *Ibid.*, p. 435.

# 8

# ACTIVITIES OF HOLY ANGELS

## Their Activities Toward God

The Scriptures reveal several activities of the holy angels toward God.

First and foremost, they worship and adore God the Father. The Apostle John saw the four beasts, 24 elders, and all the holy angels worship God the Father on His throne (Rev. 4:8-11; 5:13-14; 7:11-12). All of God's angels are commanded to praise Him (Ps. 148:2). The multitude of holy angels who appeared to the shepherds of Bethlehem praised God and ascribed glory to Him (Lk. 2:13-14).

In Bible times holy angels also occasionally communicated the will of God to human beings. For example, the angel who appeared to the women at the empty tomb on the day of Christ's resurrection told them to go quickly and tell His disciples that He had risen from the dead (Mt. 28:5-8). In addition, the angel Gabriel told Zacharias, the father of John the Baptist, what he should name his son (Lk. 1:11-13, 19) and communicated to the virgin Mary God's will for her (Lk. 1:26-38).

The third activity of the holy angels is to put what God purposes into effect by obeying His commandments (Ps. 103:20-21).

The giving of God's law to Israel through Moses at Mount Sinai was also an angelic duty. In conjunction with this, the following comments appear in the Scriptures:

> The LORD...came with ten thousands of saints. From his right hand went a fiery law for them (Dt. 33:2). (It should be noted that the word translated "saints" literally means *holy ones*. In this context it refers to holy angels, as indicated by the next biblical quotation.)

> The chariots of God are twenty thousand, even thousands of angels; the Lord is among them, as in Sinai (Ps. 68:17).

> Who have received the law by the disposition of angels, and have not kept it (Acts 7:53).

> The law...was ordained by [lit., *through*] angels in the hand of a mediator (Gal. 3:19).

> For if the word spoken by [lit., *through*] angels was steadfast, and every transgression and disobedience received a just recompense of reward (Heb. 2:2).

The language of these passages seems to indicate that God delivered the law to Moses through angelic intermediaries at Mount Sinai.

Holy angels can also administer God's judgments. For example, in David's day an angel afflicted Israel with God's pestilence judgment (2 Sam. 24:15-17). During the future seven-year

Tribulation, angels of God will administer His trumpet and bowl judgments upon the earth (Rev. 8-16).

## Their Activities Toward Jesus Christ

Holy angels have been, are, and will be actively involved in activities with Jesus Christ.

First, they worship Him. God the Father has commanded all His angels to worship Jesus Christ (Heb. 1:6). The Apostle John saw the four beasts, 24 elders, and all the holy angels worship Jesus Christ as the Lamb that was slain (Rev. 5:8-13). God the Father has highly exalted Him and given Him the highest name so that every angel—even the fallen, evil ones—will have to bow before Jesus Christ in worship and confess who He truly is (Phil. 2:9-11).

Second, the angel Gabriel foretold the supernatural conception and virgin birth of Jesus Christ (Lk. 1:26-38).

Third, an angel of God explained Mary's supernatural conception of Jesus to Joseph, her betrothed husband, and instructed him to keep her as his wife (Mt. 1:18-25). This was God's way of providing Jesus with a stable family and home during His childhood years.

Fourth, an angel announced God's choice of Jesus' human name and the fact that He would be the Savior of sinful human beings (Mt. 1:21).

Fifth, an angel announced the birth of Jesus Christ to Bethlehem shepherds. The angel asserted that his announcement was good news that was intended to bring great joy to all people. He also indicated that this announcement was good news because of who this newly born child was: a Savior, the divine Messiah (Lk. 2:8-12).

As soon as the angel had delivered his announcement, he was joined by a large host of holy angels. They praised God in the highest heaven by ascribing glory to Him and pronounced peace for human beings on earth—all because of the birth of Jesus Christ (Lk. 2:13-14).

Sixth, an angel provided for Jesus Christ's protection while He was a child. Because God knew that King Herod would try to kill Jesus, He sent an angel to Jesus' foster father, Joseph, to instruct him to take the child and His mother to Egypt until the danger was past. Once Herod died, an angel told Joseph to take the child and His mother back to Israel (Mt. 2:13, 19-20).

Seventh, holy angels ministered to Jesus Christ in His weakened physical condition after His temptation by Satan (Mt. 4:11; Mk. 1:13).

Eighth, an angel came from heaven to strengthen Jesus during His Gethsemane agony (Lk. 22:43).

Ninth, holy angels witnessed and announced Jesus Christ's bodily resurrection from the dead (Lk. 24:1-10, 22-23; Jn. 20:11-13).

Tenth, two holy angels attended Jesus Christ at His ascension into heaven (Acts 1:10-11).

Eleventh, in the future a holy archangel will accompany Jesus Christ when He comes from heaven to the air above the earth to rapture His church saints out of the world (1 Th. 4:16-17).

Twelfth, a great host of holy angels will accompany Jesus Christ in His glorious Second Coming to the earth after the future Tribulation (Mt. 24:29-31; 25:31; 2 Th. 1:7).

## Their Activities Toward Nations

During the Prophet Daniel's lifetime, a supernatural being who came to him made the following statements:

> Fear not, Daniel; for from the first day that thou didst set thine heart to understand, and to chasten thyself before thy God, thy words were heard, and I am come for thy words. But the prince of the kingdom of Persia withstood me one and twenty

days; but, lo, Michael, one of the chief princes, came to help me; and I remained there with the kings of Persia...Then said he, Knowest thou why I come unto thee? And now will I return to fight with the prince of Persia; and when I am gone forth, lo, the prince of Greece shall come. But I will show thee that which is noted in the scripture of truth; and there is none that holdeth with me in these things, but Michael, your prince. Also I, in the first year of Darius, the Mede, even I, stood to confirm and to strengthen him (Dan. 10:12-13, 20-21; 11:1).

On another occasion Daniel was told the following:

And at that time shall Michael stand up, the great prince who standeth for the children of thy people, and there shall be a time of trouble, such as never was since there was a nation even to that same time; and at that time thy people shall be delivered, every one that shall be found written in the book (Dan. 12:1).

It should be noted that the language of the supernatural being who spoke to Daniel indicated a distinction between the prince of the kingdom of Persia and the kings of Persia (Dan. 10:13). In other words, the prince was not one of the human kings of Persia.

Because the supernatural being classified Michael as a prince, because Michael helped the supernatural being fight against the prince of the kingdom of Persia (Dan. 10:13, 20-21), and because Michael is clearly identified in the Scriptures as an archangel (Jude 9), it is apparent that the prince of the kingdom of Persia was also an angel—but an evil one. The same was true of the prince of Greece (Dan. 10:20-21).

Daniel was told that Michael was his prince and the prince of the children of his people (Dan. 10:21; 12:1). This means that

Michael is the great angel whom God has assigned to the position of prince over the nation of Israel.

The term *prince* in these Daniel passages refers to powerful holy and evil angels who are assigned by God and Satan to positions of authority over nations. The holy angels are assigned by God to influence the decisions and actions of nations according to God's will. The evil angels are similarly assigned by Satan to influence the decisions and actions of nations according to Satan's will.

These passages from Daniel also reveal that these holy and evil angelic princes wage war against each other over the affairs of nations. In reference to this, Franz Delitzsch wrote, "Angels contend for the rule over nations and kingdoms, either to guide them in the way of God or to lead them astray from God."[1] The Scriptures do not reveal how they war against one another. They simply indicate that such warfare does take place.

While Persia ruled over Israel, Haman, who was strongly anti-Semitic, was advanced to a high position in the Persian government (Est. 3:1-6). He persuaded the Persian king to decree that all Jews be killed on the 13th day of the month Adar (Est. 3:7-15). The entire nation of Israel was to be annihilated in one day.

In the providence of God, a young Jewess named Esther became the favorite queen of the Persian king (Est. 2:15-17). Through her influence, the king decreed that the Jews would be permitted to defend themselves on the day of their slaughter (Est. 7; 8). The Jews did defend themselves, and as a result Israel was spared as a nation (Est. 9:1-19). Every year Jews around the world keep the feast of Purim to celebrate this deliverance from total annihilation while under Persian rule (Est. 9:20-32).

The record of these dramatic events in the Book of Esther makes no mention of angelic involvement. Two things do, however, seem apparent considering what is revealed in Daniel 10. First, ultimately the Persian decree to annihilate Israel was the result of the evil angelic prince of Persia influencing the policies of Persia. Second, the providential deliverance of Israel was the result of the heavenly being and Michael, Israel's holy angelic prince, fighting against the prince of Persia.

During part of the time that Greece, the other kingdom mentioned in Daniel 10, dominated the ancient world, Israel was brutalized by Antiochus Epiphanes, a Greek-Syrian ruler. Antiochus outlawed the Jews' worship of the God of Israel and commanded them to worship the Greek god Zeus. He plundered and defiled God's Temple, rededicated it as the Temple of Zeus, had a pagan altar built over the altar of God, and commanded that the regular sacrifices be replaced by the sacrifice of pigs. He burned and tore down large parts of Jerusalem. On several occasions he had great numbers of Jews killed and Jewish women and children sold into slavery.

Eventually the Jews were successful in liberating their nation from this Greek-Syrian oppressor and his forces. They then cleansed the Temple and restored the worship of the God of Israel. Every year Jews around the world observe the Feast of Lights (Hanukkah) to celebrate this deliverance of their nation from the brutal policies of Antiochus while under Grecian rule.

The record of this Grecian abuse of Israel and its liberation is found in the apocryphal books of 1 and 2 Maccabees. Again, a practical application of Daniel 10 is enlightening. Antiochus Epiphanes' brutal treatment of Israel was the result of the evil angelic prince of Greece influencing the policies of that kingdom. Israel's deliverance was the result of the heavenly being and Michael, Israel's holy angelic prince, fighting against the prince of Greece.

Revelation 12 indicates that during the second half of the seven-year Tribulation period, Satan will pursue Israel with a vengeance, attempting to annihilate it. For instance, toward the end of the Tribulation, Satan, the Antichrist, and the false prophet will send demons (evil angels) throughout the world to influence the rulers of all nations to bring their armed forces against Israel (Rev. 16:12-16). Because of such violent attacks against Israel, Michael will have to "stand up" in the middle of the Tribulation to go into intense action to prevent Israel's total annihilation (Dan. 12:1).[2] In the future, just as in the past, Satan and God will assign angelic princes to nations to influence their policies in favor of satanic or divine purposes for history.

Does this kind of angelic involvement with nations take place during modern times? There is good reason to conclude that it does. The era of World War II may provide an example of intense angelic involvement in international affairs. Several scholarly books and public television documentaries have chronicled the involvement of Hitler and the Nazis in the occult. Because occult practices expose people to demonic influence, it can be concluded that Hitler and the Nazis were exposing themselves to intense evil angelic influence.

Knowing that Satan assigns evil angels to nations to influence them to threaten Israel, we can understand what ultimately prompted Hitler and the Nazis to annihilate Jews through the Holocaust. Surely the utterly inhumane, systematic liquidation of some six million Jews can be explained only on the basis of demonic (evil angelic) influence.

It would appear that God assigned Michael and perhaps other holy angelic princes to fight against these evil angelic princes and to influence the allied nations to form a united force to crush Hitler and his forces.

Listening to the news, we are exposed only to the visible human element that affects the affairs of nations and international events. At the same time, we are oblivious to the very real but invisible angelic element that powerfully influences those same affairs and events and, therefore, our lives.

Sydney H. T. Page wrote:

*Bethel Baptist Church*
P.O. BOX 167
AUMSVILLE, OR  97325

The portrayal of the princes of the nations in Daniel reveals that the unfolding of human history is not determined solely by the decisions made by human beings, for there is an unseen dimension of reality that must also be taken into account. In particular, there are malevolent forces in the universe that exercise a baneful influence in the sociopolitical realm, especially where the people of God are concerned. Nevertheless, the power of these evil agencies is limited, for transcendent powers of goodness oppose them.[3]

In Matthew 24:31, Jesus Christ referred to another significant activity of holy angels toward a nation, an event that will take place in conjunction with His Second Coming as the Son of man after the Tribulation (vv. 29-30): "And he shall send his angels with a great sound of a trumpet [literal translation of the Greek text, "a great trumpet"], and they shall gather together his elect from the four winds, from one end of heaven to the other."

In this statement, Jesus referred to the future fulfillment of the prophecies in Isaiah 11:11-12 and 27:12-13. There God foretold the gathering from the four corners of the earth of the living, believing remnant of Israel at the Second Coming of the Messiah. God indicated that this gathering would happen in conjunction with the blowing of "a great trumpet" (literal translation of the Hebrew text). Thus, Jesus was teaching that holy angels will gather the nation of Israel from all over the world to its homeland at the time of His Second Coming.[4]

## Their Activities Toward the Church

The holy angels watch the church's affairs. The Scriptures indicate that this involves several tasks.

First, the angels observe what happens to church leaders. The

Apostle Paul wrote, "For I think that God hath set forth us, the apostles, last, as it were appointed to death; for we are made a spectacle unto the world, and to angels, and to men" (1 Cor. 4:9). This passage seems to indicate that angels watch the persecution, even martyrdom, of church leaders who stand fast for God's truth.

Second, angels watch what church leaders do. The Apostle Paul delivered the following charge to Timothy, a young church leader: "I charge thee before God, and the Lord Jesus Christ, and the elect angels, that thou observe these things without preferring one before another, doing nothing by partiality" (1 Tim. 5:21). This charge indicates that God the Father, Jesus Christ, and the holy angels watch how church leaders perform their responsibilities; therefore, leaders should be careful to conduct church business properly.

Third, powerful angels in the different heavens learn about God's wisdom by watching the church. In Ephesians 3:10, the Apostle Paul wrote, "To the intent that now, unto the principalities and powers in heavenly places, might be known by the church the manifold wisdom of God."

The word translated "manifold" in the expression "manifold wisdom of God" literally means "most varied."[5] In light of this meaning, Heinrich Seesemann indicates that in Ephesians 3:10 the Apostle Paul refers to the wisdom of God that has shown itself "to be varied beyond measure and in a way which surpasses all previous knowledge thereof."[6] In other words, because this wisdom of God was so unique and was not displayed until a certain point in time, even the powerful angels in the heavenly realms knew nothing about it in ages past.

Paul's statement indicates that this unique wisdom of God is now made known to these powerful angels by the church. The context of Ephesians 3:10 reveals how this is so. In the context, Paul taught that through His wisdom God had provided a way to remove the enmity that had divided Jews and Gentiles from each other in ages past—through the death of His Son, Jesus Christ (Eph. 2:11-17). As a result of Christ's death, believing Jews and Gentiles have equal access to God and are brought together in peace and as equals into one body, the church (2:15-3:9).

The point of this teaching is that only God had the unique wisdom necessary to devise a way to remove the enmity that existed for ages between Jews and Gentiles and to bring them together in peace and equality into one body. Through this wisdom, God devised this way in eternity past (Eph. 3:10-11), but that wisdom was not revealed to His creatures until believing Jews and Gentiles were brought together in that body. Thus, even the powerful angels knew nothing about this unique wisdom of God until the church came into existence after the death of Christ. Angels learn things about God's wisdom as they watch the church being built. In light of this, Ulrich Wilckens declared that this wisdom's "revelation is by the Church in which Jews and Gentiles are united."[7]

Fourth, angels are present in church worship services, watching how churches function. Paul indicated this in 1 Corinthians 11. In this chapter, the apostle gave instruction concerning proper functioning order in the worship services of churches. He introduced the proper service by first addressing the issue of proper order for men and women when they minister in public worship services.

Paul introduced this issue in verse 3 by explaining the functional authority structure that God has ordained for the universe. The functional head of Christ is God the Father; the functional head of every man is Christ; and the functional head of woman is the man.

In verses 4-16, the apostle taught the implications of this functional authority structure for men and women when they minister in a public worship service of a church. Men are not to have a covering on their heads when ministering (vv. 4, 7). By contrast, when women minister in an appropriate way publicly in a worship service where men are present, they are to have a covering on their heads (vv. 5-6).

Paul gave reasons for these distinctive roles in ministry (vv. 7-16). All of the reasons are noncultural in nature. Some of them were determined at creation before human culture existed. One of the reasons involved angels, who do not belong to human culture. "For this cause ought the woman to have authority on her head because of the angels" (v.10).

Because in verses 5-6 Paul taught that women who minister in a public worship service are to have a covering on their heads, he used the word translated "authority" in verse 10 as a synonym for that covering. Thus, in this context the apostle was indicating that the covering on the woman's head was a sign or symbol of functional authority over her.

Because the woman was to have the covering on her head, the covering symbolized the functional headship authority that God ordained for the man over the woman, as explained by the apostle in verse 3. According to Werner Foerster, two things make the meaning of verse 10 clear. First, the context indicates that "v. 10 forms part of the discussion of veiling from the one main standpoint, namely, that of the relation of woman to man."[8] Second, "regard should be had to the choice of the verb 'ought,' for in Paul this does not imply external compulsion but obligation.... It is very probable that in this verse Paul is referring to the moral duty of a woman and not to any kind of imposed constraint."[9]

In light of these two points, Werner Foerster drew the following conclusion: "The only alternative is that the veil is a sign of woman's subordination to man, i.e., that man is the head of the woman," and that is the significance of Paul's use of the word translated "authority" for the veil.[10]

It would appear, then, that the apostle was giving the following instruction: When a woman ministers publicly in a church service where men are present, she is to put this symbol of authority on her head to acknowledge that she is under the functional headship authority of the men of that church, and to indicate that she is not ministering with the motive of subverting or usurping that God-ordained functional headship authority of the men.

Because one of the reasons Paul gave for this practice was "because of the angels," we must ask the following question: What conceivable relationship could angels have to this issue? Because Paul gave this angelic reason immediately after indicating that the covering is a symbol of functional authority, it would appear that there is some connection between the issue of functional authority and angels.

The first of God's creatures to rebel against the functional authority structure that He ordained for the universe were Satan and the other evil angels. The goal of their rebellion is to overthrow God's functional headship authority over the universe so that Satan can usurp that authority from Him.

In light of this angelic rebellion, it appears that Paul's point is that God wants Christian women to be examples to angels as creatures of God who are willing to submit to His functional authority structure of the church and, in turn, the universe. This example involves their not rebelling against or trying to overthrow or usurp the functional headship authority that God has ordained for men.

This instruction by Paul implies that angels are present in church services observing how the church functions

## Their Activities Toward Individual Saints

As noted in an earlier chapter, Hebrews 1:14 states that holy angels are "all ministering spirits, sent forth to minister for them who shall be heirs of salvation." This means that God sends His angels to minister to individual saints.

Before the Scriptures were completely written, God occasionally sent holy angels as messengers to make His will known to individual saints. For example, God sent angels to make His will known to John the Baptist's father (Lk. 1:5-20), to the virgin Mary (Lk. 1:26-38), and to Joseph (Mt. 1:18-25; 2:13-21).

There are at least three ways in which holy angels have ministered to individual believers in the past and continue to do so today.

First, angels guard and preserve saints. Psalm 91:10-12 promises that God gives His angels charge over His people to guard and protect them from harm. The Bible records several instances of God's keeping this promise. For example, the Lord sent angels to deliver Lot and his family from the destruction of Sodom (Gen. 19:1-25). He sent an angel to protect Daniel from the fury of the lions (Dan. 6:16-22). He sent an angel to set the apostles and Peter free from imprisonments (Acts 5:17-20; 12:1-11).

A veteran missionary tells of an experience she had during a terrorist uprising in the nation where she served. One night while she was in bed in the rear room of the two-room house in which she lived, a terrorist came running through the front doorway with a machete in his hand. When he reached the open doorway to her bedroom, he slammed into a barrier. The man staggered back in a daze. He then tried to run through the open doorway again but experienced the same result. He furiously lashed the open space of the doorway with his machete, but there was nothing there. As a result, he tried to run through the doorway a third time but again ran into an invisible but solid barrier. He finally gave up attempting to enter her bedroom and left. Neither the terrorist nor the missionary saw anything but empty space in the doorway. The missionary concluded that a holy angel blocked that doorway to protect her from harm.

Such experiences, both in the past and present, prompt the question: Is each individual believer assigned his or her own personal guardian angel for life? Perhaps so. It appears that the early Jewish church saints believed this to be true. After Peter's release from prison, he went to the home of John Mark and his mother, where believers were holding a prayer meeting. After a young woman heard Peter at the gate, she interrupted the meeting by announcing that Peter was there. The believers insisted that it was not Peter, but "his angel" (Acts 12:12-15). Their use of the possessive pronoun "his" seems to indicate that they believed that Peter had his own personal angel.

On one occasion, when Jesus talked about little children, He referred to "their angels" in heaven (Mt. 18:10). His use of the possessive pronoun "their" may imply that each child has his or her own personal angel.

The issue of whether or not each person is assigned his or her own guardian angel for life is really not that important. What is crucial is the fact that each person who inherits salvation is guarded and preserved through angelic activity, whether it be by one or several angels, throughout life. When believers get to glory, they may be amazed to learn how many times in this earthly life angelic protection kept them from harm or premature physical death.

Second, holy angels assist the prayers of saints. The Apostle John saw angels in heaven having golden bowls filled with the prayers of saints and an angel offering incense with the prayers of all saints upon the golden altar before God's throne (Rev. 5:8; 8:3). These sights seem to indicate that holy angels gather together the prayers of saints in heaven and offer them as a sweet smelling offering to God. In that sense, they assist the prayers of saints.

In addition, a holy angel freed Peter from prison while church saints were praying. It appears that angels execute some of God's answers to the prayers of saints (Acts 12:1-12).

Third, holy angels carry the souls of dead saints to heaven. In Jesus' account of Lazarus and the rich man, He declared that when Lazarus died, angels carried him into Abraham's bosom

(Lk. 16:22). It would appear, then, that today, when the soul of a saint is separated from his or her body at death, angels transport that soul into the presence of the Lord in heaven. This means that a believer is not left alone at death. Because of this angelic ministry to saints, Paul stated that to be absent from the body is to be present with the Lord (2 Cor. 5:8).

These significant ministries of angels to saints prompt the conclusion that we are indebted to them, but even more so to God for sending them to minister to us. This is another aspect of God's grace toward us.

## Their Activities Toward Unbelievers

The activities of holy angels toward unbelievers are primarily, if not exclusively, activities of judgment. For example, cherubim prevented fallen man from having access to the tree of life in the Garden of Eden (Gen. 3:24). Angels played key roles in the judgment of Sodom and Gomorrah (Gen. 19:10-25). An angel inflicted a fatal illness upon King Herod Agrippa I because he accepted the ascription of deity to himself by some of his subjects (Acts 12:20-23). Holy angels will administer God's trumpet and bowl judgments upon the unbelieving world of the Tribulation period (Rev. 8-18). At the Second Coming of Christ to earth immediately after the Tribulation, His angels will remove all living unbelievers from the earth and cast them into a horrible place of judgment (Mt. 13:24-30, 36-43, 47-50; 24:29-31, 37-41; 25:31-46).

## ENDNOTES

[1] Franz Delitzsch, *Biblical Commentary on the Prophecies of Isaiah*, Vol. I, trans. by James Martin (Grand Rapids: Wm. B. Eerdmans Publishing Company, 1960), p. 434.

[2] For a fuller description of this persecution and Michael's preserving ministry, see Renald E. Showers, *The Most High God* (Bellmawr, NJ:  The Friends of Israel Gospel Ministry, Inc.,

1982), pp. 170-72.

[3] Sydney H. T. Page, *Powers of Evil* (Grand Rapids: Baker Books, 1995), p. 64.

[4] For an in-depth explanation of Matthew 24:31, see Renald E. Showers, *Maranatha: Our Lord, Come!* (Bellmawr, NJ: The Friends of Israel Gospel Ministry, Inc., 1995), pp. 181-184.

[5] Heinrich Seesemann, "polupoikilos," *Theological Dictionary of the New Testament,* Vol. VI, ed. by Gerhard Friedrich, trans. and ed. by Geoffrey W. Bromiley (Grand Rapids: Wm. B. Eerdmans Publishing Company, 1968), p. 485.

[6] *Ibid.*

[7] Ulrich Wilckens, "sophia," *Theological Dictionary of the New Testament*, Vol. VII, ed. by Gerhard Friedrich, trans. and ed. by Geoffrey W. Bromiley (Grand Rapids: Wm. B. Eerdmans Publishing Company, 1971), p. 523.

[8] Werner Foerster, "exousia," *Theological Dictionary of the New Testament*, Vol. II, ed. by Gerhard Kittel, trans. and ed. by Geoffrey W.Bromiley (Grand Rapids: Wm. B. Eerdmans Publishing Company, 1964), p. 573.

[9] *Ibid.*, p. 574.

[10] *Ibid.*

## 9

# ACTIVITIES OF
# EVIL ANGELS

### Their Activities Toward God

There are at least two primary activities of evil angels toward God. First, they oppose God. Throughout history they have tried to defeat His will, and they continue to seek to overthrow Him as the ultimate sovereign of the universe. Satan, when he began his revolt against God, asserted that he would make himself like the Most High, the ultimate sovereign. Evil angels war against holy angels whom God appoints to influence the policies of nations in accord with His will. Satan repeatedly hindered the Apostle Paul from returning to the Thessalonian saints to perform God's ministry there (1 Th. 2:18). There is no doubt that evil angels work to hinder God's servants from executing His ministries in the world today.

Second, sometimes when evil angels actively try to thwart

God's will, they actually perform His will. For example, when Satan attacked Job to try to get him to curse God, he actually accomplished God's will. God wanted Job tested to demonstrate a truth to His enemy, Satan. Thus, Elmer B. Smick, referring to Satan as the accuser and Job's adversary, wrote the following based upon the record in Job 1:

> It is not the Accuser but the Lord who initiates the testing of Job; for the Lord says: "Have you considered my servant Job? There is no one on earth like him" (v. 8). God's statement that Job is his servant implies more than mere servitude; it means God and Job are in a covenant relationship based on solemn oaths.... Here the Lord sees fit to use secondary means to accomplish his purpose. That purpose is not just to test Job as an end in itself but to give Job the opportunity to honor his Lord to whom he has pledged his allegiance with a solemn oath. That allegiance becomes a significant part of the cosmic struggle between Job's adversary and the Lord. Will Job curse God or not? . . . The Accuser insinuates that Job's allegiance is hypocritical (v. 9). If only God would remove the protective hedge he has placed about Job (v. 10), this "devout" servant would certainly curse God to his face. The attack is on God through Job, and the only way the Accuser can be proven false is through Job.[1]

Another example of an evil angel accidentally serving God's will is found in 1 Corinthians 5. A man in the church in Corinth was persistently living in an open, scandalous, illicit sexual relationship (v. 1). It is apparent that the man refused to stop this sinful practice. God could not permit one who was known as a Christian (v. 11) to continue defaming the names of God and

Christ before the world. Thus, Paul, as an authoritative apostle of Christ, determined to turn this man over to "Satan for the destruction of the flesh [premature physical death]" (vv. 3-5). Apparently this persistent, unrepentant sin fit the category of what the Apostle John called "a sin unto death" (1 Jn. 5:16). Surely Satan would love to have permission to inflict physical death upon a believer and thereby rid the earth of a child of God; however, his infliction of death upon the man in 1 Corinthians 5 would have been a service to God.

Paul gave a third example of an evil angel actually doing God a service while attacking one of His servants (2 Cor. 12). Because Paul had been given so many revelations from God, he was in danger of becoming very proud. Pride would have crippled the effectiveness of God's ministry through him; therefore, Paul was subjected to a trying infirmity. He described his situation as follows: "And lest I should be exalted above measure through the abundance of the revelations, there was given to me a thorn in the flesh, the messenger of Satan to buffet me, lest I should be exalted above measure" (v. 7).

The word translated "messenger" in the expression "messenger of Satan" also means *angel*. This may imply that Satan inflicted this infirmity upon Paul through one of his evil angels.

On three different occasions Paul asked the Lord to remove this infirmity from him, but the Lord refused to do so (vv. 8-9). This refusal indicates that it was the Lord's will for His servant to have this infirmity so that the effectiveness of God's ministry through him would not be hindered through pride.

Concerning Paul's affliction, Murray J. Harris wrote:

> It is remarkable that Paul could regard his affliction as given by God and yet as "a messenger of Satan." This may support the view that the affliction was some type of physical malady, because in 1 Corinthians 5:5 (cf. 1 Cor 11:30; 1 Tim. 1:20)

Satan appears as God's agent for the infliction of disciplinary illness (cf. Job 2:1-10).[2]

All three of these examples illustrate important principles. Satan and his evil angels cannot attack one of God's children without God's permission. When God grants that permission, evil angels are limited strictly to what He permits. They may not go beyond the boundaries He sets. Finally, when God grants His permission, He does so for a good purpose.

## Their Activities Toward Saints

As was made clear by these three examples from Job, 1 Corinthians 5, and 2 Corinthians 12, it is evident that evil angels attack saints. In addition to these specific examples, other biblical passages indicate the same truth.

In Ephesians 6:11-13, the Apostle Paul gave the following commands to believers:

> Put on the whole armor of God, that ye may be able to stand against the wiles of the devil. For we wrestle not against flesh and blood, but against principalities, against powers, against the rulers of the darkness of this world, against spiritual wickedness in high places. Wherefore, take unto you the whole armor of God, that ye may be able to withstand in the evil day, and having done all, to stand.

The expression "the wiles of the devil" refers to the deceptive methods Satan uses to try to gain advantage over saints in spiritual warfare.[3] Satan is not powerful enough to defeat God in a head-on conflict, but he is more powerful and intelligent than God's people are by themselves. Thus, in order to strike at God, Satan tries to lead saints into sin through the art of seduction. God's people cannot withstand the deceit of Satan alone; therefore, God has provided means whereby they can keep their ground against the enemy's superior power and intelligence (v. 11).

In verse 12 Paul explained why believers must put on the whole armor of God. They are in spiritual conflict with supernatural beings. Paul used a present tense verb to indicate that this conflict is continuous throughout this life. The word translated "wrestle" reveals the nature of the conflict. It comes from a verb that means *to swing* or *to throw*, and refers to a wrestling match in which two parties battle until one opponent throws the other down on his back and pins him.[4] The apostle indicated that the believers' opponents in this spiritual war are not mere human beings. His description of these opponents indicates that they are powerful evil angels who dwell in one of the heavens.

Paul made it clear that these evil angels are the wicked rulers of the moral, spiritual darkness that characterizes the present world system. By contrast, believers are full of light and are to live as children of light (Eph. 5:8). When they live that way, they are testimonies of God's light to the humans whom Satan holds in darkness. Satan hates this testimony of light; therefore, he sends his evil angels to battle against the saints, to try to prevent them from living as children of light. This is a battle between two kingdoms: God's kingdom of light and Satan's kingdom of darkness.

In this passage, then, Paul was teaching that the saints are in a constant battle against Satan's evil angelic host. As human beings, believers are not able to stand firmly against these supernatural attackers without supernatural aid. Thus Paul commands the saints to avail themselves of God's armor.

Another passage that indicates that evil angels attack the saints is Romans 8:37-39. In this passage Paul declared,

> Nay, in all these things we are more than conquerors through him that loved us. For I am persuaded that neither death, nor life, nor angels, nor principalities, nor powers, nor things present, nor

> things to come, Nor height, nor depth, nor any
> other creation, shall be able to separate us from the
> love of God, which is in Christ Jesus, our Lord.

In these statements, Paul listed things that we might think would have the potential of separating true believers from God's love. For some of those things he used terms that refer to demons or evil angels. Paul was implying that evil angels attack believers with the goal of separating them from God's love. The apostle made it very clear, however, that the evil angels can never accomplish that goal because of what Christ has done for us. Thus, when commenting on this passage, Everett F. Harrison wrote, "Demons are evil spirits such as those often mentioned in the Gospels. Being agents and underlings of the devil, they would delight to separate Christians from Christ, but they cannot do so."[5]

Third, the Apostle Peter warned believers to "Be sober, be vigilant, because your adversary, the devil, like a roaring lion walketh about, seeking whom he may devour; Whom resist steadfast in the faith, knowing that the same afflictions are accomplished in your brethren that are in the world" (1 Pet. 5:8-9).

Fourth, Satan accuses the saints before God when they sin (Rev. 12:10).

Fifth, Satan tempts the saints to sin (1 Cor. 7:5; 1 Th. 3:5).

Sixth, Satan uses various devices to "get an advantage" of believers (2 Cor. 2:11).

Seventh, Satan demands that God permit him to sift or test (put through trials) the saints to try to get their faith to fail.[6] He did this with Job (Job 1; 2) and Peter and his companions (Lk. 22:31-32; the "you" in verse 31 is plural in the Greek text).

Eighth, Satan sets snares or traps for church leaders, which, if fallen into, will nullify or destroy the effectiveness of God's ministries through them (1 Tim. 3:7).

Not only do Satan and his evil angels attack the saints, but also, either directly or through his angels, Satan sometimes uses believers to do his work. For example, Satan provoked David to take a census of Israel and thereby stir up God's wrath against the nation (1 Chr. 21:1-7). He used Peter as his mouthpiece to try to persuade Jesus to avoid His death on the cross (Mt. 16:21-23). Satan prompted Ananias and Sapphira to lie to the Holy Spirit (Acts 5:1-11).

## Their Activities Toward Satan

The evil angels support Satan in his plans and purposes; therefore, they attempt to carry out his wishes. This is indicated by the fact that he is called "the prince of the demons" (Mt. 9:34; 12:24) and "the prince of the power of the air" (Eph. 2:2). These titles indicate that Satan has ruling authority over the host of evil angels (Mt. 25:41; Rev. 12:7-9).

## Their Activities Toward Unbelievers

Satan and his evil angels carry on a number of activities toward unbelievers. First, Satan exercises dominion over the world system, which includes all of the unsaved. Jesus indicated this by calling him "the prince of this world" (Jn. 12:31; 14:30; 16:11). Satan had the authority to offer Jesus the rule of the world system (Lk. 4:5-7). For this reason John declared that "the whole world lieth in wickedness" (1 Jn. 5:19), and James warned believers not to be a friend of the world system (Jas. 4:4).

Second, Satan functions as the spiritual father of the unsaved (Jn. 8:44). As a result, all of the unsaved are his spiritual offspring or children (Mt. 13:38-39; 1 Jn. 3:10).

Third, Satan tries to prevent the unsaved from becoming saved by snatching away the Word of God that was sown in their hearts (Mt. 13:19), blinding their minds against the gospel (2 Cor. 4:3-4), leading the whole world astray by deception (Rev. 12:9), having his evil angels devise false doctrines (1 Tim. 4:1), disguising himself as an angel of light (2 Cor. 11:14)[7], and using false teachers who disguise themselves as apostles of Christ and ministers of righteousness (2 Cor. 11:13-15).[8] In the future, he will hold on to many unsaved people by enabling the Antichrist and the false prophet to display supernatural power, signs, wonders, and unrighteous deception. Through these means, many will be duped into acknowledging and worshiping the Antichrist as God (2 Th. 2:9-10; Rev. 13).

Fourth, evil angels (demons) are involved with every false religion (religions that do not require the worship of one true God—the personal, sovereign, creator God of the Bible). Several biblical passages indicate this.

Deuteronomy 32:12-18, where Israel is called "Jeshurun" (see Isa. 44:1-2), describes the tragic spiritual decline of the nation. After the people of Israel had been blessed by God with great material prosperity, they began to feel so self-sufficient that they "kicked" against the idea that they should remain in a right relationship with Him (vv. 12-15). As a result, they "forsook," "lightly esteemed," became "unmindful" of, and forgot God (vv. 15, 18). Then they provoked Him to jealousy and anger by worshiping false gods and adopting the abominable practices of the false religions related to those gods (v. 16). Verse 17 clearly indicates that when they offered sacrifices to the gods of those religions, in reality they offered them to "demons" (evil angels). This involvement in false religions provoked God's anger to the point that He promised to bring terrible judgments upon Israel (vv. 19-29).

The next passage indicating that evil angels are involved with false religions is Psalm 106:35-38. It describes how the people of Israel adopted the idolatrous religions of the pagan Gentiles in the land of Canaan (v. 35). In their service to the idols of those religions, the Israelites even adopted the pagan practice of child sacrifice, a practice that God hates and calls an abomination (Dt.

12:31). They shed the "innocent blood" of their own children by offering them as sacrifices on the altars of "the idols of Canaan" (v. 38). Verse 37 states that the Israelites thereby "sacrificed their sons and their daughters unto demons" (evil angels). This stirred the wrath of God so strongly that He judged the nation of Israel severely through its foreign enemies (vv. 40-43). What does this say for a nation whose people sacrifice their children on the altars of personal expediency, convenience, and selfishness through abortion and infanticide?

The third passage that reveals the involvement of evil angels with false religions is 1 Corinthians 10:19-20. In verse 19, Paul declared that the idols in false religions amount to nothing. They are simply material objects that can't do a thing by themselves. In verse 20, however, the apostle indicated that evil, supernatural beings are involved in the religions related to idols. He made it clear that sacrifices offered to idols are, in reality, offered to "demons," and therefore those who eat a sacrificial meal at a pagan worship place become companions or partners of the demons related to that false religion (the word translated "fellowship" in verse 20 means "companion, partner, sharer"[9]). In light of this teaching by Paul, Werner Foerster wrote, "Demons stand behind paganism."[10]

In the next passage, Paul reminded the Corinthian Christians that when they were pagan Gentiles, they were "carried away unto these dumb idols, even as ye were led" (1 Cor. 12:2). According to Charles Hodge, this comment indicated that in conjunction with their past false religions, the Corinthians "were controlled by an influence which they could not understand or resist."[11] W. Harold Mare identified that influence when he wrote, "Paul implies that the Corinthians had experienced the effects of evil spirits in their former pagan worship."[12]

Because the Corinthians were Greeks, research into ancient Greek religions sheds light on Paul's comment. The goal of participating in some of those pagan religions was temporary union of the human worshiper with one of the gods or goddesses.[13] The belief was that such union could take place either by the worshiper's soul temporarily leaving his or her body to unite with the deity, or by the deity temporarily entering and taking control of the worshiper's body. Erwin Rohde stated,

> This belief was that a highly exalted state of feeling could raise man above the normal level of his limited, everyday consciousness, and could elevate him to heights of vision and knowledge unlimited; that, further, to the human soul it was not denied, in very truth and not in vain fancy, to live for a moment the life of divinity.[14]

During that experience, the person was controlled by a supernatural power. Rohde referred to it as:

> the enthusiasm and exaltation that overwhelmed the senses and enthralled the will and consciousness of those who gave themselves up to the powerful Dionysiac influence. Like an irresistible current that overwhelms a swimmer or like the mysterious helplessness that frustrates the dreamer, the magic power emanating from the neighborhood of the god took complete possession of the worshipper and drove him whither it willed. Everything in the world was transformed for him; he himself was altered.[15]

Drugs were one means of inducing these experiences, but according to Rohde, "The means most commonly adopted by such peoples to produce the desired intensity and stimulation of feeling is a violently excited dance prolonged to the point of exhaustion, in the darkness of night, to the accompaniment of tumultuous music."[16]

He related an example of this means:

> The festival was held on the mountaintops in the
> darkness of night amid the flickering and uncer-
> tain light of torches. The loud and troubled sound
> of music was heard; the clash of bronze cymbals;
> the dull thunderous roar of kettledrums; and
> through them all penetrated the "maddening uni-
> son" of the deep-toned flute, . . . Excited by this
> wild music, the chorus of worshippers dance with
> shrill crying and jubilation. We hear nothing
> about singing: the violence of the dance left no
> breath for regular songs. . . It was in frantic,
> whirling, headlong eddies and dance-circles that
> these inspired companies danced over the moun-
> tain slopes.[17]

The worshipers would continue this wild dance until a supernatural power would seize and take control of them. When it did
seize them, it frequently produced cannibalism through them.

> In this fashion they raged wildly until every sense
> was wrought to the highest pitch of excitement,
> and in the "sacred frenzy" they fell upon the beast
> selected as their victim and tore their captured
> prey limb from limb. Then with their teeth they
> seized the bleeding flesh and devoured it raw.[18]

> In Greece the awful god received the blood of
> human victims. Nor did the outward signs of
> delirious frenzy, such as the eating of raw flesh,
> the killing and tearing in pieces of snakes, entire-
> ly disappear.[19]

In light of biblical revelation concerning the activities of
demons, it is obvious that these worshipers were being seized and
controlled by demons (evil angels) in conjunction with their
pagan religions. Missionaries and Christians from several
nations have related the same activities and results they have wit-

nessed personally among 20th-century worshipers of non-Christian religions. In each instance, it has involved the same type of music and dancing that the ancient Greeks used to induce their demonic experiences. In light of this, is it just coincidence that the 20th-century Western world has experienced an explosion of paganism and demonic, occultic influence and practices, including ritual sacrifices and raw cannibalism because this same kind of music has invaded its shores?

The final passage related to the involvement of evil angels with false religions is Revelation 9:20. It indicates that idol worshipers of the future Tribulation period will actually be worshiping "demons" (evil angels).

Fifth, Satan uses unsaved individuals as counterfeit believers and false teachers to infiltrate local churches and other ministries (Acts 20:28-31; Gal. 2:4-5; 2 Pet. 2:1-3; 1 Jn. 2:18-19; Jude 3-4). Through this means, he hopes to destroy or nullify the effectiveness of these ministries by perverting the gospel, causing divisions, introducing wrong practices, and compromising, diluting, or adulterating God's truth. First Timothy 4:1 reveals that false teachers are the instruments of demons (evil angels). It indicates that "seducing spirits" (evil spirits who try to lure people away from God's truth) work through false teachers, and that demons are the source of false teaching ("doctrines of demons," teaching contrary to the Scriptures; see also 2 Tim. 3:13; 2 Pet. 2:1-3).

Sixth, evil angels (demons) take possession of some unsaved human beings (Mt. 8:16, 28-31; 9:32; 12:22; 15:22; 17:14-18).

Seventh, Satan, either directly or through his angels, uses unsaved humans to do his work (including murder) in the world. For example, Satan prompted Cain to commit the first murder in history (Jn. 8:44; 1 Jn. 3:12). He prompted unsaved enemies of Jesus to try to kill Him (Jn. 8:40-44). Satan entered into Judas to motivate him to betray Jesus (Lk. 22:3-6; Jn. 13:2; 6:70-71). Satan prompts unsaved people to lie (Jn. 8:44; Rev. 3:9), blaspheme (Rev. 2:9), cast believers into prison (Rev. 2:10), kill saints (Rev. 2:10, 13), and oppose presentations of the gospel to prevent other unbelievers from becoming saved (Acts 13:6-10).

Eighth, during the future Tribulation period, Satan will try to destroy Israel, including all unsaved Jews. In Revelation 12 the Apostle John recorded two divinely revealed signs. One was "a great red dragon" (v. 3), which represented Satan (v. 9). The other was a woman who was clothed with the sun, stood on the moon, had a crown of 12 stars on her head, and gave birth to a son who was caught up to God in heaven and would eventually rule all the nations with a rod of iron (vv. 1-2, 4-5).

The sign of the woman is based on imagery found in the Old Testament. There Israel is portrayed as a woman (Isa. 54:5-6; Ezek. 16:7-14); Jacob (whom God renamed Israel) is portrayed as the sun; Rachel, his wife, is portrayed as the moon, and Jacob's sons, the heads of the 12 tribes of Israel, are portrayed as stars (Gen. 37:9-10). This imagery indicates that the woman in Revelation 12 represents the nation of Israel through which the Messiah, who will rule the nations with a rod of iron (Ps. 2:7-9; Rev. 19:15), was born.

Revelation 12 teaches that the dragon (Satan) will persecute the woman (Israel) [v. 13], that Israel will flee to a wilderness area to escape this persecution (vv. 6, 14), and that Satan will try to destroy Israel (v. 15). This attempt by Satan to destroy Israel will last for 1,260 days (v. 6) or "a time, and times, and half a time" (v. 14). In other words, it will last for three and one-half years. The time terminology in verse 14 is found in Daniel 7:25 and 12:7, where it refers to the second half of the seven-year Tribulation period. In light of this, it appears that Revelation 12 is indicating that Satan will try to destroy Israel, including all unsaved Jews, during the second half of the Tribulation period.

Why will Satan try to destroy all unsaved Jews during that time period? Because of the following program to which God is committed:  God will not fully crush Satan, remove him and his evil kingdom rule from the earth, and restore His own theocratic kingdom rule to this planet until unsaved Israel repents (Zech. 12-14; Acts 3:12-21).[20]

In light of this divine program, Satan thinks that because unsaved Israel must repent before God will crush him, if he (Satan) can destroy unsaved Israel before it repents, then God will never crush him.

In the middle of the future Tribulation period, Satan and all his fallen, free angels will be cast from their heaven to the earth and confined there (Rev. 12:7-9).  This will alert Satan to the fact that his time is growing short.  As a result, he will go after unsaved Israel with great wrath, trying to destroy it before it can repent (Rev. 12:12-13).

Ninth, during the future Tribulation period, Satan will empower and use two unsaved men—the Antichrist and the false prophet—to try to establish a visible, worldwide, political form of his kingdom rule on the earth, to form a new false religion (worship of the Antichrist as God) and deceive many people into adopting that religion, to try to destroy all witness for God, and to try to destroy Israel (Dan. 7:7-8, 19-26; 9:26-27; 11:36-45; 2 Th. 2:3-12; 1 Jn. 2:18; Rev. 13; 19:19-20).

Tenth, near the end of the Tribulation period, Satan, the Antichrist, and the false prophet will send evil angels (demons) throughout the world to prompt the unsaved rulers of the nations to bring their armies into the land of Israel (Rev. 16:12-16).  Satan will have two reasons for drawing the military might of the entire, unsaved Gentile world to that location at that time.

He will hope that it can help him prevent the Second Coming of Christ to the earth.  Satan knows that he and his rule of the world system will be crushed if Christ succeeds in returning.  In addition, he knows that the land of Israel will be the first place to which Christ will return in His Second Coming (Zech. 14:3-5).

Thus, Satan will have the Gentile world's rulers and armies gathered there under his Antichrist and false prophet to oppose Christ and His army at His coming (Rev. 19:11-21).

Then, Satan will hope that through the combined military might of the unsaved Gentile world, he will be able to totally annihilate unsaved Israel before it can repent. Although this force will succeed in destroying two-thirds of the Jews, it will fail to annihilate the final one-third (Zech. 13:8). That one-third remnant will survive what, in scope, will be Israel's worst holocaust and will repent (Zech. 13:9; 12:9-13:1).

Eleventh, after the thousand-year reign of Christ and the saints over the earth, Satan will lead all of the unsaved who are alive on earth at that time in a final but unsuccessful revolt against that rule (Rev. 20:4-10).

# ENDNOTES

[1] Elmer B. Smick, "Job," *The Expositor's Bible Commentary*, Vol. 4, ed. by Frank E. Gaebelein (Grand Rapids: Zondervan Publishing House, 1988), p. 880.

[2] Murray J. Harris, "2 Corinthians," *The Expositor's Bible Commentary*, Vol. 10, ed. by Frank E. Gaebelein (Grand Rapids: Zondervan Publishing House, 1976), p. 396.

[3] F. F. Bruce, *The Epistle to the Ephesians* (Fleming H. Revell Company, 1961), p. 127.

[4] A. T. Robertson, *Word Pictures in the New Testament*, Vol. IV (New York: Richard R. Smith, Inc., 1931), p.550.

[5] Everett F. Harrison, "Romans," *The Expositor's Bible Commentary*, Vol. 10, ed. by Frank E. Gaebelein (Grand Rapids: Zondervan Publishing House, 1976), p. 100.

[6] Ernst Fuchs, "siniadzo," *Theological Dictionary of the New Testament*, Vol. VII, ed. by Gerhard Friedrich, trans. and ed. by Geoffrey W. Bromiley (Grand Rapids: William B. Eerdmans

Publishing Company, 1971), pp. 291-92.

[7] William F. Arndt and F. Wilbur Gingrich, *A Greek-English Lexicon of the New Testament* (Chicago: The University of Chicago Press, 1957), p. 515.

[8] *Ibid.*

[9] *Ibid.*, p. 440.

[10] Werner Foerster, "daimon," *Theological Dictionary of the New Testament*, Vol. II, ed. by Gerhard Kittel, trans. and ed. by Geoffrey W. Bromiley (Grand Rapids: Wm. B. Eerdmans Publishing Company, 1964), p. 17.

[11] Charles Hodge, *The First Epistle to the Corinthians* (London: The Banner of Truth Trust, 1959), p. 240.

[12] W. Harold Mare, "1 Corinthians," *The Expositor's Bible Commentary*, Vol. 10, ed. by Frank E. Gaebelein (Grand Rapids: Zondervan Publishing House, 1976), p.261.

[13] Erwin Rohde, *Psyche: The Cult of Souls and Belief in Immortality among the Greeks* (New York: Harcourt, Brace & Company, Inc., 1925), p. 258.

[14] *Ibid.*, p. 291.

[15] *Ibid.*, p. 286.

[16] *Ibid.*, p. 261.

[17] *Ibid.*, p. 257.

[18] *Ibid.*

[19] *Ibid.*, p. 285.

[20] For a full explanation of this divine program, see Renald E. Showers, *What on Earth is God Doing?* (Neptune, NJ: Loizeaux Brothers).

# 10

# THE ANGEL OF THE LORD

The Old Testament Scriptures refer to a being who, on several occasions, either appeared (Jud. 6:12; 13:3) or spoke (Gen. 22:11, 15; 31:11) to human beings. This being had several titles applied to him in many passages, some of which are listed below:

- **"the angel of the LORD"** (Jehovah or Yahweh, Gen. 16:7, 9-11; 22:11, 15; Ex. 3:2; Num. 22:22-27, 31-32, 34-35; Jud. 6:11-12, 21-22; 13:3, 13, 15-18, 20-21)
- **"the angel of God"** (Elohim, Gen. 21:17; 31:11; Ex. 14:19; Jud. 6:20; 13:6, 9)
- **"the captain of the host of the LORD"** (Josh. 5:14-15)

An examination of the Old Testament references to this being reveals that he was a divine being, not an angelic creature of God. It should be noted that the word translated "angel" in the Bible means *messenger* and sometimes refers to beings other than

angels.[1]   For example, it was used for Jesus' and John the
Baptist's disciples when they were sent out as messengers (Lk.
9:52; 7:24).   In light of this, the fact that the being referred to
above was called "the angel of the LORD" and "the angel of God"
does not require the conclusion that he was an angelic being.

## Evidences of Deity

We shall examine several of the Old Testament references that
indicate the deity of the angel of the LORD.

**The Angel and Hagar**:  The angel of the LORD ministered on
two different occasions to Hagar, Sarai's handmaid (Gen. 16:7-
13; 21:17-18).   Three things in the records of these occasions
reveal his deity.  First, he declared that he would multiply Hagar's
descendants exceedingly (16:10) and would make a great nation
from her son Ishmael (21:18).   Only deity could cause those
things to happen.  Second, Hagar called the angel of the LORD
"God" (16:13).   Third, Moses, who recorded these occasions,
called this being "the LORD [Jehovah or Yahweh]" (16:13).
Moses would never apply this most sacred name of deity to anyone who was not a divine being.

**The Angel and Abraham**:  The angel of the LORD spoke to
Abraham (Gen. 22:11-18).   God tested Abraham's faith by com-
manding him to take his only son Isaac to the land of Moriah and
offer him there as a burnt offering (vv. 1-2).   In obedience,
Abraham took Isaac to that land, built an altar, laid his son on it,
and prepared to kill him.  Because Abraham had passed the test
of his faith through these actions, the angel of the LORD called out
to him from heaven before he could kill Isaac.  He commanded
Abraham not to kill his son and said, "now I know that thou fear-
est God, seeing thou hast not withheld thy son, thine only son
from me" (vv. 11-12).   Through this statement, the angel of the
LORD indicated that he was the one from whom Abraham had not

withheld his son and therefore was the one who had commanded him to sacrifice Isaac. Because it was God who had given that command (vv. 1-2), the angel of the LORD was thereby equating himself with God.

**The Angel and Jacob**: The angel of the LORD interacted with Jacob more than once. When he spoke to Jacob as the angel of God in a dream, he told him that he was "the God of Bethel" (Gen. 31:11-13).

Through this statement concerning Bethel, the angel of the LORD was referring to another dream Jacob had years earlier (Gen. 28:12-19). In that dream, the LORD (Jehovah or Yahweh) stood above a ladder that reached to heaven. He spoke to Jacob, declaring that He was "the LORD God [Jehovah Elohim] of Abraham, thy father, and the God [Elohim] of Isaac," and making promises that only deity could fulfill (vv. 12-15). When Jacob woke from that dream, he said, "Surely the LORD [Jehovah or Yahweh] is in this place" and "This is none other but the house of God" (vv. 16-17). These conclusions prompted him to name that place Bethel (*house of God*) [v.19].

When the angel of the LORD stated that he was the God of Bethel, he thereby was claiming that He was Jehovah Elohim, the LORD God of Abraham and Isaac, the one who could fulfill the promises that only deity could fulfill.

It should be noted that Hosea 12:4-5 identifies the being who interacted with Jacob at Bethel as "the LORD God of hosts" (Jehovah Elohim Sabaoth) and "the angel."

On another occasion, "a man" wrestled with Jacob all night and "prevailed not against him" (Gen. 32:24-30). Although the text does not say so, several things indicate that this "man" was the angel of the LORD and deity. First, in light of Hebrews 7:7, which says that "the less is blessed of the better," it appears that this man was greater than Jacob because Jacob wanted him to bless him (v. 26), and the man did bless him (v. 29).

Just as God had the authority to change the names of Abram and Sarai (Gen. 17:5, 15), so this man had the authority to change Jacob's name to "Israel" (v. 28). The name Israel means "he contends with God."[2] The man who assigned this new name to Jacob explained the reason for this choice. Through Jacob's wrestling with and prevailing against him, Jacob had contended with and prevailed against God (v. 28). In other words, this man was God. But in what sense could Jacob, a mere man, prevail against God? J. Barton Payne gives the following explanation:

> The name *yisrael* was bestowed upon Jacob by the Angel of Yahweh himself, after he had wrestled with him all night (Gen. 32:24). Jacob's struggle was spiritual, in prayer (Hos. 12:4), as well as physical. And in it the patriarch "prevailed." Not that Jacob defeated God, but that he finally attained God's covenantal requirement of yielded submission (dramatically signalized by his injured thigh, Gen. 32:25). And he persisted in refusing to let the Angel go until he had blessed him (v. 26).[3]

Jacob recognized that this man was deity. This is evident because after his episode with this man, he named the place of wrestling "Peniel" (which means "face of God"[4]) because he had "seen God face to face" (v. 30). In addition, he expressed grateful surprise that he had survived the encounter alive (v. 30).

Hosea 12:3-5, referring to this incident of Jacob's wrestling with this man and seeking his blessing, states, "by his [Jacob's] strength he had power with God. Yea, he had power over the angel, and prevailed; he wept, and made supplication unto him." Through this statement, this passage identifies the man who wrestled with Jacob as "God" (Elohim) and "the angel."

When Jacob, near the end of his life, blessed Joseph's sons, he stated, "God, before whom my fathers, Abraham and Isaac, did walk, the God who fed me all my life long unto this day, An angel who redeemed me from all evil, bless the lads" (Gen. 48:15-16). Through that statement, Jacob identified the angel of the LORD with God (Elohim).

**The Angel and Moses:**  The angel of the LORD appeared to Moses in the fire of the burning bush (Ex. 3:2-4:17). Many things in this passage indicate the deity of the angel of the LORD.

Several times he is called "the LORD" (Jehovah or Yahweh) [3:4, 7; 4:2, 4, 6, 11, 14] and "God" (Elohim) [3:4, 6, 11, 13, 14, 15, 16; 4:5].

The angel of the LORD called himself "I AM" (3:14). This was a claim of absolute deity.

"The angel of the LORD appeared unto him in a flame of fire out of the midst of a bush" (3:2), and "God called unto him out of the midst of the bush" (3:4). It is obvious that these two statements refer to the same being.

The same verse (3:2) declares that the angel of the LORD appeared to Moses, but 3:16 and 4:5 state that it was the LORD God of Abraham, Isaac, and Jacob who appeared to him.

Several things also indicate that this man was the LORD.

The angel of the LORD made the following claim about himself: "I am the God of thy father, the God of Abraham, the God of Isaac, and the God of Jacob" (3:6).

In response to that claim, "Moses hid his face; for he was afraid to look upon God" (3:6). This action indicates that Moses recognized the deity of the angel of the LORD.

The angel of the LORD told Moses to remove his shoes because the land upon which he stood near the burning bush was holy ground (3:5). The Scriptures imply that everywhere God is uniquely present is holy (see Isa. 57:15; Ps. 5:7; 47:8; Ex. 19:10-25). Thus, the fact that the ground around the burning bush was holy indicates that God was present there in a unique sense. In line with this, C. F. Keil and Franz Delitzsch wrote, "The place of the burning bush was holy because of the presence of the holy God."[5] Thus, it was God, not a created angel, who was present in the burning bush.

The angel of the LORD called the children of Israel "my people" (3:7, 10). In other passages, the LORD God also called them "my people" (e.g., 2 Chr. 6:4-5). The combination of these passages indicates that the angel of the LORD was the LORD God.

The angel of the LORD said that he came to deliver the people of Israel out of their affliction in Egypt (3:8, 17). In other passages, the LORD God said that He was the one who brought them out of Egypt (e.g., 2 Chr. 6:4-5). Once again the combination of passages identifies the angel of the LORD with the LORD God.

The angel of the LORD said that he would smite Egypt with wonders (3:20). Other passages indicate that it was the LORD who did this (e.g., Ex. 19:3-4; Dt. 29:2-3).

**The Angel and Israel**: In Exodus 14:19-20 Moses wrote that the angel of God accompanied the people of Israel with the pillar of cloud and fire. However, in Exodus 13:21-22 he stated that it was the LORD (Jehovah or Yahweh) who accompanied them with the pillar. It seems obvious that Moses thereby equated the angel of God with the LORD.

Two significant things concerning the angel of the LORD and Israel should be noted from Isaiah 63:9. First, the angel is called "the angel of his presence." The pronoun "his" refers back to "the LORD" (Jehovah or Yahweh) in the immediately preceding context (vv. 7-9a); therefore, Isaiah was equating the angel of the LORD with the LORD's presence. Second, Isaiah declared that the angel of his presence "saved" the people of Israel (v. 9), but immediately before that declaration he stated that the LORD was Israel's "Savior" (vv. 7-8). Through both of these statements Isaiah was insinuating that the angel of the LORD is the LORD.

In Judges 2:1-5, the angel of the LORD rebuked the people of Israel for making alliances with Canaanites. He claimed that he was the one who had vowed to their ancestors to give the land of Canaan to Israel, had brought the people of Israel out of Egypt into Canaan, and had made a covenant with Israel (v. 1). Other passages clearly indicate that it was the LORD who did all these things regarding Israel (Gen. 13:14-17; 15:18; 17:1-2, 7-8; 26:1-3; 28:10-15; Dt. 26:8-9; 29:1-9). Thus, through his comments the angel of the LORD identified himself as the LORD. In light of this, C. F. Keil and Franz Delitzsch stated, "The person who appeared to the people was not a prophet, nor even an ordinary angel, but *the angel of the Lord*, who is essentially one with Jehovah."[6]

**The Angel and Balaam**: Numbers 22:31-35 records the angel of the LORD's appearance to Balaam with his sword drawn in his hand. He told Balaam, "only the word that I shall speak unto thee, that thou shalt speak" (v. 35). But Numbers 23:5 states that "the LORD put a word in Balaam's mouth?" In addition, it is apparent that Balaam recognized that the angel of the LORD was the LORD God because he said, "The word that God putteth in my mouth, that shall I speak" (Num. 22:38); "Must I not take heed to speak that which the LORD hath put in my mouth?" (23:12); and "All that the LORD speaketh, that I must do" (23:26). Combining all of these statements with what the angel of the LORD told Balaam indicates that the angel of the LORD is the LORD God.

**The Angel and Joshua**: A unique man appeared to Joshua near Jericho (Josh. 5:13-15). Although the text does not say that the person who appeared was the angel of the LORD, several things indicate that he was that being.

This man appeared with his sword in his hand, just as the angel of the LORD did when he appeared to Balaam. This man identified himself as the "captain of the host of the LORD" (lit., "the prince of the army of Jehovah, i.e. of the angels," see 1 Ki. 22:19; Ps. 103:20-21; 148:2[7]). This indicated that he was a heavenly warrior in authority over all the holy angels; therefore, although he appeared in the form of a man, he was not a human being.

Although Joshua himself was a great warrior, he recognized that this person was superior to him. He fell on his face before him, worshiped him, called him "my lord," and referred to himself as this person's servant.

This man told Joshua to remove his shoes because the place where he stood was holy. The angel of the LORD told Moses to do this, and for the same reason, at the burning bush.

The presence of this unique person made the ground where Joshua stood holy. As noted earlier in observations related to Moses' burning bush experience, it is the unique presence of God that makes a location holy.

In Joshua 6:2, this person is called "the LORD."

This person asserted that he had given the Canaanite city of Jericho into Joshua's hand (6:2). According to Joshua 1:1-3, it was the LORD who promised to give the land of Canaan to the Israelites. Taken together, these passages imply that this person was the LORD.

**The Angel and Gideon:** The angel of the LORD appeared to Gideon and commissioned him to lead the Israelites in driving out their Midianite oppressors (Jud. 6:11-24). Several things indicate the deity of the angel of the LORD.

First, he is called "the LORD" twice (vv. 14, 16).

Second, the angel of the LORD told Gideon, "Surely I will be with thee, and thou shalt smite the Midianites" (v. 16). Later Gideon stated that it was God who said He would save Israel by Gideon's hand (v. 36). This indicates that eventually Gideon recognized the deity of the angel of the LORD.

Third, when Gideon realized that it was the angel of the LORD who had appeared to him, he was afraid of dying (vv. 22-23). Because people in Old Testament times knew that death was possible for a mortal human who saw deity (Ex. 3:6; 19:21; 1 Ki. 19:13), Gideon's reaction revealed his belief in the deity of the angel of the LORD.

**The Angel and Samson's Parents**: The angel of the LORD appeared first to Samson's mother and later to both of his parents (Jud. 13:1-23). Once again, several things reveal the deity of this being. The angel of the LORD said that his name was "Wonderful" (v. 18). C. F. Keil and Franz Delitzsch indicated that this was not the proper name of the angel of the LORD. Instead, it was an adjective describing the nature of his name. Concerning this word, they stated, "It is to be understood in an absolute sense— 'absolutely and supremely wonderful.' "[8] Because names in Bible times were designed to reveal the nature of their bearers, Keil and Delitzsch pointed out that just as the name of the angel of the LORD was absolutely and supremely wonderful in nature, so his own nature was wonderful in that same sense.[9] Because only divine nature is wonderful in the absolute, supreme sense, Keil and Delitzsch asserted that in this passage the word "wonderful" is used "as a predicate belonging to God alone."[10] Thus, when the angel of the LORD said that his name was wonderful, he thereby declared his deity.

Samson's father indicated that he and his wife saw God when they saw the angel of the LORD (v. 22). He thereby asserted the deity of this being.

Samson's father, like Gideon, expressed the fear that he and his wife would die as the result of seeing the angel of the LORD (v.22). As noted earlier, people in Bible times had this fear when they were convinced that they had seen deity.

## The Identification of the Angel of the Lord

**A Significant Distinction**: Through these examples, it is apparent that the angel of the LORD was clearly identified with the LORD (Jehovah or Yahweh) God (Elohim) in Old Testament times. He was a divine being possessing absolute deity, not an angelic being.

It should be noted, however, that some Old Testament passages indicated a distinction between the LORD God and the angel of the LORD. In a lengthy passage (beginning with Ex. 20:1) in which God spoke to the people of Israel as "the LORD thy God" (20:1-2), He made the following statements:

> Behold, I send an angel before thee, to keep thee in the way, and to bring thee into the place which I have prepared. Beware of him, and obey his voice, provoke him not; for he will not pardon your transgressions; for my name is in him. But if thou shalt indeed obey his voice, and do all that I speak; then I will be an enemy unto thine enemies, and an adversary unto thine adversaries. For mine angel shall go before thee, and bring thee in unto the Amorites, and the Hittites, and the Perizzites, and the Canaanites, the Hivites, and the Jebusites; and I will cut them off (Ex. 23:20-23).

The fact that the LORD God said He sends this angel indicates that He and this angel were distinct from each other. They were not the same being. This same distinction was given again in Exodus 32:33-34 and 33:1-2.

Because the LORD God sent this angel "before" Israel, and because it was the angel of the LORD who went "before" Israel (Ex. 14:19), it is apparent that the angel whom the LORD God sent was the angel of the LORD.

Because the LORD God and the angel whom He sent before Israel were distinct from each other, and because the angel whom He sent was the angel of the LORD, we can conclude that the LORD God was distinct from the angel of the LORD. They were not the same being.

In addition to the statements concerning the LORD God's sending His angel before Israel, there is another biblical indication of this distinction.  Several people in Old Testament times saw the angel of the LORD, but centuries later the Apostle John stated, "No man hath seen God at any time" (Jn. 1:18; 1 Jn. 4:12).  This contrast draws a distinction between the angel of the LORD and the being whom John called God.

**Important Questions**:  We have seen extensive evidence for the deity of the angel of the LORD.  The Old Testament clearly identified him with the LORD God.  But we also have noted biblical indications of a distinction between the angel of the LORD and the LORD God who sent him—the being whom John called God.  They were not the same being.

This contrast prompts some important questions.  How can the angel of the LORD be the LORD God and yet be a distinct being from the LORD God who sent him?  Is this a contradiction?

God's inspired Scriptures never contradict themselves; therefore, we must conclude that this is not a contradiction

**The Explanation**:  In the Old Testament, there is more than one being who is God, possessing absolute deity.  This is indicated in several ways.

First, Psalm 45:7 states, "therefore God, thy God, hath anointed thee with the oil of gladness above thy fellows."  Here one being who is God (Elohim) calls another being God (Elohim).

Second, the Old Testament indicates that God had a Son. Psalm 2:7 records the LORD (Jehovah or Yahweh) saying to another being, "Thou art my Son."  After a series of questions concerning God as the Creator, Proverbs 30:4 asked, "what is his son's name…?"  Isaiah 9:6 foretold that God would give His Son.

These Old Testament references to God's having a Son are very significant because the term *son* signifies that a son has the same nature as his father.  In the Old Testament and writings of post-biblical Judaism, the Hebrew words for *son* were "often used to denote the relationship which determines the nature of a man."[11] In light of this, the fact that God has a Son means that there is another being who has the same divine nature as God. Thus, one being with absolute deity is the Father, and the other being with absolute deity is the Son.

Third, concerning the Son whom God would give, Isaiah 9:6 declared that His name would be called "The Mighty God." Franz Delitzsch declared that this name "attributes divinity" to the Son.[12]

Fourth, in Jeremiah 23:5-6 one being who is "the LORD" (Jehovah or Yahweh) calls another being "the LORD" (Jehovah or Yahweh).

Because the Old Testament mentions two distinct beings who are God, possessing absolute deity, we can conclude that one of those beings is the LORD God who sent the angel of the LORD before Israel, the Father who would give His Son, the God whom no man has seen. We can also conclude that the other being is the angel of the LORD, the Son who would be given by the Father and who had the same nature as the Father.

**The Specific Identification**: The angel of the LORD can be more specifically identified with Jesus Christ. There are several reasons for this conviction.

First, we noted earlier that the angel of the LORD was the "I AM" who met with Moses at the burning bush. Jesus Christ declared that He was the "I am" (Jn. 8:58).

Second, it has been concluded that the LORD God who sent the angel of the LORD was the divine Father and that the angel of the LORD was the divine Son. Jesus Christ claimed that God was His Father and that He Himself was the Son of God (Jn. 5:19-37; 10:36-38). The Jews recognized that Jesus' claim to be the Son of God was a claim of equality with God (Jn. 5:18).

Third, the angel of the LORD had the same divine nature as the

LORD God who sent him before Israel. Jesus Christ declared that
He and the Father were one in nature (Jn. 10:30). The Jews realized that He thereby was claiming to be God (absolute deity) [Jn.
10:31-33].

Fourth, the LORD God who sent the angel of the LORD before
Israel stated that His name was in Him (Ex. 23:21). Jesus Christ
said that He came in His Father's name (Jn. 5:43).

Fifth, the angel of the LORD was the Son who would be given
by God the Father. The Scriptures indicate that Jesus Christ is the
Son whom God the Father gave to the world (Jn. 3:16, Gal. 4:4;
1 Jn. 4:9).

Sixth, when the angel of the LORD appeared to Joshua, he iden-
tified himself as the captain of the host (angelic army) of the
LORD. Jesus Christ is sovereign over the angels. At His Second
Coming, He will lead the angelic army out of heaven (Mt. 25:31;
Rev. 19:14).

Seventh, the angel of the LORD told Samson's parents that his
name was "Wonderful" in nature. Isaiah 9:6 indicated that the
name of the Messiah, the Son whom God would give, would be
called "Wonderful." It seems apparent from this that the angel of
the LORD was the Messiah. Jesus Christ claimed to be the
Messiah (the Christ) [Jn. 1:41; cp. Jn. 4:25-26; 10:24-25], and
others recognized that He was the Messiah (Mt. 16:16; Lk. 4:41;
Jn. 4:42).

Eighth, the angel of the LORD accompanied the people of Israel
in their exodus journey out of Egypt to the land of Canaan. In 1
Corinthians 10:1-9, the Apostle Paul asserted that it was Christ
who accompanied them in that journey. Charles Hodge wrote the
following concerning Paul's assertion:

> The rock that followed them was Christ. The
> Logos, the manifested Jehovah, who attended the
> Israelites in their journey, was the Son of God who
> assumed our nature, and was the Christ. It was he

> who supplied their wants....This passage distinct-
> ly asserts not only the preexistence of our Lord,
> but also that he was the Jehovah of the Old
> Testament.  He who appeared to Moses and
> announced himself as Jehovah, the God of
> Abraham, who commissioned him to go to
> Pharaoh, who delivered the people out of Egypt,
> who appeared on Horeb, who led the people
> through the wilderness, who dwelt in the temple,
> who manifested himself to Isaiah, who was to
> appear personally in the fulness of time, is the per-
> son who was born of a virgin, and manifested him-
> self in the flesh.  He is called, therefore, in the Old
> Testament, an angel, the angel of Jehovah,
> Jehovah, the Supreme Lord, the Mighty God, the
> Son of God—one whom God sent—one with him,
> therefore, as to substance, but a distinct person.[13]

C. F. Keil and Franz Delitzsch expressed the same viewpoint:

> The Angel of Jehovah, therefore, was no other
> than the Logos, which not only "was with God,"
> but "was God," and in Jesus Christ "was made
> flesh" and "came unto His own" (John 1:1-2, 11);
> the only-begotten Son of God, who was *sent* by
> the Father into the world, who, though one with
> the Father, prayed to the Father (John 17).[14]

In light of these statements, we can conclude that Jesus Christ
was the divine angel of the LORD in the Old Testament, manifest-
ing Himself before His incarnation.

## ENDNOTES

[1] William F. Arndt and F. Wilbur Gingrich, *A Greek-English
Lexicon of the New Testament* (Chicago: The University of
Chicago Press, 1957), p. 7.

[2] J. Barton Payne, "yisrael," *Theological Wordbook of the Old Testament*, Vol. II, ed. by R. Laird Harris, Gleason L. Archer, Jr., and Bruce K. Waltke (Chicago: Moody Press, 1980), p. 883.

[3] *Ibid.*

[4] "Peniel," *The New International Dictionary of the Bible*, ed. by J. D. Douglas and Merrill C. Tenney (Grand Rapids: Zondervan Publishing House, 1987), p. 762.

[5] C. F. Keil and Franz Delitzsch, *The Pentateuch*, Vol. I, in *Biblical Commentary on the Old Testament* (Grand Rapids: Wm. B. Eerdmans Publishing Company, 1959), pp. 439-40.

[6] C. F. Keil and Franz Delitzsch, *Joshua, Judges, Ruth* in *Biblical Commentary on the Old Testament* (Grand Rapids: Wm. B. Eerdmans Publishing Company, 1960), p. 266.

[7] *Ibid.*, p.62.

[8] *Ibid.*, p. 407.

[9] *Ibid.*

[10] *Ibid.*

[11] Eduard Lohse, "huios," *Theological Dictionary of the New Testament*, Vol. VIII, ed. by Gerhard Friedrich, trans. and ed. by Geoffrey W. Bromiley (Grand Rapids: Wm. B. Eerdmans Publishing Company, 1972), p. 358.

[12] Franz Delitzsch, *Biblical Commentary on the Prophecies of Isaiah*, Vol. I (Grand Rapids: Wm. B. Eerdmans Publishing Company, 1960), p. 252.

[13] Charles Hodge, *An Exposition of the First Epistle to the Corinthians* (London: The Banner of Truth Trust, 1959), p. 175.

[14] C. F. Keil and Franz Delitzsch, *The Pentateuch*, Vol. I, p. 191.

# More Books by
## Renald E. Showers

**MARANATHA: OUR LORD, COME!**
*A Definitive Study of the Rapture of the Church*
This in-depth study addresses such issues as the Day of the Lord, its relationship to the Time of Jacob's Trouble and the Great Tribulation, the 70 Weeks of Daniel, and much more. Learn why the timing of the Rapture has practical implications for daily living and ministry.
ISBN 0-915540-22-3, #B55P

**THERE REALLY IS A DIFFERENCE!**
*A Comparison of Covenant and Dispensational Theology*
Learn how theological differences affect such issues as God's ultimate purpose for history, God's program for Israel, the church, and the Christian's relationship to the Mosaic Law and grace. This excellent book also explores the differences between the premillennial, amillennial, and postmillennial views of the Kingdom of God and presents an apology for the dispensational-premillennial system of theology.
ISBN 0-915540-50-9, #B36

## THE MOST HIGH GOD

One of the finest commentaries on the book of Daniel available today, this clear, concise, and consistently premillennial exposition sheds tremendous light on prophecy, the Times of the Gentiles, and other portions of the prophetic Word.
ISBN 0-915540-30-4, #B26

## TWO MILLENNIA OF CHURCH HISTORY

This comprehensive, easy-to-understand, and beautifully illustrated 24-page booklet puts 2,000 years of church history at your fingertips. An exceptional resource, it will enable you to trace the development of first-century Orthodoxy, Romanism, the Reformation, liberal theology, the great spiritual awakenings, and much, much more.
ISBN 0-915540-67-3, #B82

## THE FOUNDATIONS OF FAITH
### Volume 1

This is a compiliation of Dr. Showers' in-depth studies in systematic theology. *The Revealed and Personal Word of God* is the first in the series and covers bibliology and Chrisology—the doctrines of the Bible and the Messiah. This hardback, fully indexed volume is a must for any serious student of God's Word.
ISBN 0-915540-77-0, #B89